OG NIHAL ART HANAYAKE CHILDREN
LISA BATTY MARK BAXTER STEPHEN
K LEE BOFKIN SAM LOYD
UTTERFLY MARK CH DEL
TER CRAGG EMILY C KY
NGTON LEIGH DICKINSON HELEN M
ROUGH BEN ELLIOT SUZETTE FIELD
BLE GRANT GILLESPIE IVO GORMLEY
RAY DAME ZAHA HADID LAL HARDY
SON ANYA HINDMARCH LEON HO
OPKINS POPPY JACKSON NORMAN
SS JULIA BOBBY KASANGA BERNIE
Y JAMES LAVELLE CIARA LAWRENCE
HA COLEMAN ROBERT LORDAN BIB
Y BILL MCLACHLAN TATIANA MERCER
LETT NASH RUPERT NEWMAN DAVID
E PILKINGTON KATE POLAND JEMIMA
AND JOLYON RUBINSTEIN NAZNEEN
JALI Q RAÚF EMMA RICE THE LORD
ROGERS RUTH ROGERS EKATERINA
PHIL RYAN JASON SANDY CHARLES
ANDRA STAVROU VINEGAR STROKES
HOMAS CHARLOTTE TILBURY SETH
AMS MARTINE WRIGHT PETER YORK

CONRAD GAMBLE

FOR THE

Olivia Big Ed
Grant Ade Gray Phil Ryan
John Pearse Deyan Sudjic James Birch
Stephen Bayley Mark Baxter Noel Clarke
Emma Rice Bernie Katz Dame Zaha Hadid
Tatiana Mercer
Stephen Fry Micky Henry Holland
Dawg
Norman Jay Bobby Kasanga Roger Anne Maningas
Peter York
Sadie Coles Mavity Don Letts
Heydon Prowse & **LOVE** Nazneen Rahman
Jolyon Rubinstein Dom Joly
Simon Russell Beale Nihal Arthanayake
Dylan Jones Ruth Rogers Martine Wright
Sir John Hegarty
Valerie Brandes Fergus Henderson
Lee Bofkin Sir Paul Smith
Anya Hindmarch Lloyd Bradley
Pauline Black
Lord Richards
And Many
More

OF
LONDON

For my father, who loved books
and loved London.

—

CONRAD GAMBLE

FOR THE

Olivia Grant · Big Ed · Ade · Gray · Phil Ryan · James Birch
John Pearse · Deyan Sudjic · Mark Baxter · Noel Clarke
Stephen Bayley · Dame Zaha Hadid
Emma Rice · Bernie Katz · Tatiana Mercer
Stephen Fry · Micky Dawg · Henry Holland
Norman Jay · Bobby Kasanga · Roger · Anne Maningas
Peter York · Mavity · Don Letts
Sadie Coles
Heydon Prowse & Jolyon Rubinstein

LOVE

Nazneen Rahman
Dom Joly
Simon Russell Beale · Nihal Arthanayake
Dylan Jones · Ruth Rogers · Martine Wright
Sir John Hegarty
Valerie Brandes · Fergus Henderson
Lee Bofkin · Sir Paul Smith
Anya Hindmarch · Lloyd Bradley
Pauline Black
Lord Richards
And Many
More

OF

LONDON

WHAT MAKES LONDON GREAT BY THE PEOPLE WHO MAKE IT GREAT

Contents

Introduction

Not long ago, on a balmy summer's evening, I sat behind an adorable little girl on a coach to Heathrow. She was glued to, and worryingly enraged by, her smartphone. Her aunt took it away and suggested she might want to look out of the window, as they "weren't in London often" and "you never know what you might see". The girl could not even finish her complaint before her eyes widened as she caught a glimpse of the extraordinary Natural History Museum. Soon, question after wonder-filled question spilled out of her as she steamed up the window with her nose pressed against the glass. "I love London," she exclaimed. "I 'specially like the lights."

When I was that little girl's age – six or so – I vividly remember being enthralled by the size of Battersea Power Station as we drove over the Thames at night. As there was nothing to compare it with, I could never gauge the size of it, which always excited and scared me in equal measure. Around the same time my father used to take my brother and me to the greasy spoon down the road from my mother's gallery near Russell Square. Hearing ol' Tony, the café's larger than life Italian proprietor, talk and gesticulate about the Old Country, sitting among couriers, suits and labourers alike and hearing their diverse patter, gave me a buzz for London that has never left me. That was, until my father died, a few years ago. After that, the music of the London streets seemed to die for me, too. So I moved away, to Barcelona. A wonderful city, a magical time. But after a while I realised it wasn't London. London's wit and wonder were things I couldn't stay parted from. On my return I decided to celebrate this pillar of tolerance, this festival of culture, this melting pot of humanity.

Discussing with Stephen Fry about how, when the graves of the original settlers of Londonium were excavated, the bones were found to belong to people from many different places. He tapped his chin, looked at me and said "and thus was ever so".

Benjamin Disraeli once remarked that "London is a roost for every bird." With over 300 languages spoken by tongues from nearly every nation on Earth, as well as being one of the few major cities that has social housing in all of its boroughs, London can be considered a modern-day Babel.

I have walked the streets from Wimbledon to Wapping, from Harrow to Hackney, from South Ken to Stratford, and it seems to me that Dr Johnson was right when he said, "There is in London all that life can afford." Because it is hectic and sleepy. It is old and modern. It is green and urban. It is noisy and peaceful. It is traditional and cutting edge. It is brash and sophisticated. It rumbles underground and rises to the sky.

London is an epic story, with glorious locations that make your heart race and your head think. And, like all the best stories, it has wonderful characters. This book is filled with those characters and their favourite aspect of this phenomenal place. From leaders in their fields to those who are the local lifeblood. I wanted people whose beat helped set the rhythm of London. Their brief was simple: to reveal something that captivated them, something they were in love with about London. There is, therefore, a diverse range of vignettes that furnish this book and capture parts of London you may not know but may come to adore.

So this is a love letter to the city, and it is real love, because I know you have your faults and, despite those, London, I love you so.

Conrad Gamble

Big Ade

Actor and hustler

LONDONER NO 1

Listen… The phone call that turns everything on its head. You know that phone call, don't you…? The call that turns your mood – *my* mood – from A to Z. Upside down. You know that phone call. Right?

I get one of those calls every day. *If I don't get one of those calls, I'm winning.*

"Often heard, rarely seen." You might say this description fits me. I've had many nicknames and professional titles over the years: from the "Under Mayor of London Town" to "character actor" spanning *Snatch* and *Casino Royale* (007). I just seem to find myself in the middle of things. Right time, wrong place…? Always have done.

I didn't grow up in Central London. I moved here when I was 18 or so. Previously, I'd visited as a youngster with my Mama. She was the best woman in the world. We used to travel all around town using a Red Bus Rover, sort of an equivalent to today's Travelcard. She took me to Trafalgar Square and I'd be climbing up those giant lions. I loved them lions. We travelled everywhere using this pass, which may well be how I got my lasting taste for movement, for *motion*: understand?

If there's one thing that defines me, and there's many things, but one thing has been constant throughout my life, from the time I was riding the bus with my Mom all the way up to right now, to last night, even; when I was tooling around town in the comfort of my car, covering a zone reaching from Hackney to Chelsea and points in between. With my friend of the day beside me, part of the time. Just cruising around town before and after midnight: popping in *here*, dropping in *there*. It's *movement* that drives me. It's driven my whole life.

Born in North London. At age 18, Central London became my home, and soon enough the entire city became my manor. I don't mean just one or two neighbourhoods. No way. I mean the whole metro area: from Hackney to Heathrow. *Greater* London… It's all my *manor*; that is, if you want to use words like that: words which most people who use 'em don't properly understand… You know why I got the keys to the whole city? Because I'm always moving, and respectful to existing cultures in that particular manor, that's why. No neighbourhood is foreign to me.

I love and embrace it all, the *whole* city.

As a teenager I loved the various music genres emerging from the UK. I'd come to realise London really was the Mecca for all bands and artists, I loved Siouxsie and the Banshees, the Jam, Pete Wylie and the Clash – it was punk and other movements. From early on, even then, I'd frequently be inside recording studios. Moving with the music. I remember early years, growing up, seeing the words "CLASS WAR" tagged over the walls of my 'hood. In the background, however, there was always music. Always music… The great leveller. *Movements* and *music*. They were key for me then and they remain key for me now. I moved forward in time with the music.

From one movement to the next, one place to another. Keeping moving. *That's* what gets Ade going.

I relocated from the East End to the West End in the late '80s. I moved right into the heart of the city. That year proved to be auspicious timing. The same time I moved to town, something big was happening in our country. It was a game-changer, 1988. The birth of acid house. It was chaos, but it was creative chaos. I was hanging with musical legends on sabbaticals. We loved this city. Acid house was a musical movement and a social movement too. It mobilised the youth.

Nowadays, the young… You see 'em and – they've got *no movement*. Nothing to flock to. So instead, it's like: "Let's all of us grow a beard!" I feel sorry for them, honestly.

Soho has always been my central. And it's still central to my life. I go there for my suits, to this day. To John Pearse on Meard Street – another Soho legend. No, a *British* legend. Not only is he my tailor but, as I keep on discovering, he's the tailor of many outstanding Englishmen, from global rock stars to… No. I'm not giving names out, are you kidding?

Looking back across my time in London, I feel some pride. My familiar zone inside the city, if I'm pressed to define it, stretches from Old Street and Clerkenwell to Seven Sisters to Bow. A big zone, admittedly. I love the 24-hour supermarkets you get here and nowhere else. It's like a mini-Berlin today, the area around Hackney. Although you'll just as easily find me in Royal China on Baker Street or Bayswater – you'll find me in the West End, if I'm pursuing film stuff!

London is best at night-time when all are asleep, roads are empty, a ghost town. My favourite area to experience this is the Embankment. It's simply magical – the illuminated buildings and bridges are quite something, driving around listening to Sam Cooke…

London's past identity was strong, it was and is a melting pot for all-comers. I look at the youth today: what major movements have they got to belong to?

Oh, I know! The movement of having no money. In a city they are increasingly priced out of, by global rich kinds with plenty of the stuff.

Ameer Ahmed

Digital journalist apprentice at the BBC

SHOREDITCH

I was born, raised and still live there today, Shoreditch, the East End of London.

If (for some weird reason) I was asked what Shoreditch tastes like, I would say a pizza. Like the dough it is the perfect base, being located close to the City, shouldering East London boroughs. But, as with a pizza, the toppings make it unique and for me it is the many people that pass through there every day, the architecture and the overall atmosphere that make it what it is.

I am one of those people who enjoy pineapple on a pizza and that topping best describes the people of Shoreditch – bright, exotic and fresh. It's the people who make the area, from the residents to the business owners to the general public passing through. It would be a very broad statement for me to say everyone in Shoreditch is nice, but the vibe and emotion you get of people bounces up the High Street, putting a smile on faces. Outsiders may describe Shoreditch as a very hipster place and I can see why, but the afternoon of 30 April 2015 sent out a message. A very popular Grime UK artist, Skepta, made a surprise announcement on Twitter that in a couple hours he was going to do a free show in Shoreditch under a tunnel. I went down there thinking, "He's only given people a two-hour warning to get to this show,

there will probably be hardly anyone coming." I was wrong. Hundreds of kids, teenagers and adults from many ethnicities swarmed the streets of Shoreditch, trying to cram under this tunnel that is generally used by homeless people to sleep. The atmosphere was electric and it was nice to see so many people enjoying themselves, but due to health and safety hazards it wasn't very long before the surprise show got "shut down" (no pun intended).

I once described Shoreditch as the Las Vegas of London, and maybe that was a bit of an exaggeration, but for me it is (I have never been to Las Vegas). The strip of shops, buildings and artwork paints the mood and creates this vibrant atmosphere that allows Shoreditch to live up to its recent reputation.

Another aspect of Shoreditch I find amazing is the culture and mix of people. There are loads of food, clothing and hairdresser shops from all different backgrounds, whether you're going to the Mexican stall for a burrito or to a Turkish-style barber's, I sometimes forget I am only in Shoreditch and not on the Copacabana beach (I have never been to the Copacabana beach).

And if it is not obvious that I love Shoreditch, when I turned 18 we became even closer – now I know why I called it the Las Vegas of London.

Andy Hank Dog

Rock 'n' roll zelig

8 NUGGETS OF SOUTH LONDON CLAY

LOCK IN
It had been the Easy Come 24th anniversary at Skehans – a little Irish pub in Nunhead – up in the hills and under the radar – the fans blow the smoke around, but the curtains and windows stay shut

London's longest running acoustic club and its moveable feast – Ivy House, Old Nun's Head, White Horse Peckham – has hosted Wednesdays. Pubs gentrify but there is always one more old-school boozer to reign in my domain

HANDBAG
Guys shooting left-handed pool make you feel like gals – "No, take it again." Started wearing a handbag this summer – freedom pass, Ray-Bans, American spirits, pre-rolled colour-coded weed and hash, clipper spex in a small under-armpit Lacoste – the shirt-top pocket won't fit all this paraphernalia

BOOT
Virtually everything comes from Pimlico car-boot: 11.30 Sundays, then back along the river – through the park to Battersea boot – today I am looking for a size 16 cool black pleated skirt, a kilt and some casual traditional Japanese men's attire

SLICE OF REALITY
Crimson dusk and the meridian laser arches overhead – disappearing past Hilly Fields Stone Circle and on to Camelot – an ancient moat in Barnet

Dixie can swing that gangplank like a seasoned salty matelot, but dogs can't climb the ladders between the decks

My 65th aboard this wondrous unique millennial artwork on stilts

E-BIKE
Take the Hibbit over Clapham Common on my Infineum electric bike – my girlfriend calls it a mobility scooter – that whipplington lurcher can run like an arrow from a bow

SUBTERRANEAN
I'm gonna throw a party in Jack Cade's Cavern under Blackheath – part of a huge network of caves and tunnels that lead to Chislehurst – then onto Coldrum Stones and Kit's Coty, the Medway Megaliths. Alternatively I could locate Merlin's cave beneath Penton Hill Clerkenwell Filthy McNasty's

FUNK SKUDGE
We are in bed by 9.30am after a scarlet sunrise speeding on some shit coke and a chunk of skunk fudge – Ese is still enjoying the balcony, firing off astonishing sweet riffs from the old strange racket box

MARGARET FINCH
Three hundred years ago the gipsy queen of Gipsy Hill would sit on her haunches all day, telling fortunes as charcoal smouldered – 108 when she died and couldn't be laid flat, so they buried her in a box

"Old Margaret Finch she's still on her haunches to this day when the worms twist her bones in the cold wet South London clay"

Nihal Arthanayake

Radio and TV presenter; Trustee of the Southbank Centre

MY LONDON

Rather than limit myself to one spot, I have to be greedy and talk about three places that I love in London. One involves spoiling myself with a great meal, one reflects my love of menswear and the third is an idyllic haven of calm in one of London's off-the-radar parks.

Starting with food, I'd like to tell you about the place I go to for a posh curry. There is of course a time and a place for a subcontinental stew: a bright red mess with an oil slick placed upon it (minus dying seabirds) and some pillow-sized naans, all washed down with a gallon of lager. The time is 2am and the place is Brick Lane. But when it comes to a massage of all your culinary senses there's only one Indian restaurant you should go to. This temple to Indian cuisine is called Benares and I am a devotee.

Located above the Bentley showroom in Berkeley Square, Mayfair, the location alone tells you that you are not in for the type of clientele that stagger in, slump into their seat and in a slur ask for the hottest thing on the menu. As the doormen usher you in and you ascend the dark staircase, the sublime aromas just waft around you. The Chef Patron Atul Kochhar has had his Michelin star for ten years and you can understand why. The layers of flavouring, subtlety of colour and carefully orchestrated presentation make every dish an event. The staff are all well informed and friendly, so no matter how you are dressed or how complicated the dish, the welcome and experience are always top-notch.

Make sure you try some of the cocktails too. The mixtures of East and West contained within your glass you won't find anywhere else, and on paper should not work. Trust me, they do. Rather too well.

Shopping for menswear can be an intimidating experience. I no longer wish to be confronted by some lithe, square-jawed narcissist asking me if there's anything I would like in a tone that says there's nothing that I can afford. It's so naff. I always feel like saying, "Relax, pal, you didn't design the clothes." That is why I love shopping on Lamb's Conduit Street, a gloriously village-like street just a five-minute walk from Holborn in Central London. If you want to dress really well, and avoid the stuffiness and eye-watering prices of Savile Row and the rather staid conservativeness of Jermyn Street, then head to Lamb's Conduit Street. From British designers like Universal Works and Folk to the more streetwear-focused Content Store which carries a number of brands, Lambs (as it is abbreviated to) is a place for those who feel that style supersedes fashion. It is also a street that exudes calm, so even if you don't have a subscription to GQ you won't feel intimidated by the thought of shopping there.

My favourite shop on Lambs, though, is Oliver Spencer. There's rarely a day goes by that I am not wearing something of his and the

store is a peaceful place to browse without the hassle of an over-attentive shop assistant or the frantic nightclub-meets-clothing-supermarket that defines a visit to a West End department store's menswear zone. The atmosphere in Lambs reminds me of a village High Street: I have even seen guys from some of the shops come out and play cricket on a balmy summer afternoon.

If London is the menswear capital of the world, then Lamb's Conduit Street is the place to go to understand why London has achieved that status.

Before I've had some retail therapy at Oliver Spencer or posh grub at Benares, a morning walk with my dog is the order of the day. London has a myriad of parks. There are the fashionable ones such as Hyde, Regent's, Queen's, Victoria and so on; and then there are those unfashionable ones that I think of as the state schools of parks.

They are utilitarian and speak of some socialist ideal made verdant. They point you towards doing rather than contemplating. In my part of Northwest London there is Gladstone Park, a lush, hilly, rolling slab of greenery situated between Dollis Hill and Neasden. An outdoor gym, basketball and tennis courts, football and rugby pitches, two playgrounds and a duck pond serve the population well. But at the very top of the park there is a walled garden which in spring and summer is a beautifully maintained carnival of flora and fauna. It feels like a secret garden taken straight from a Victorian novel. It doesn't seem to belong there, like a baroque painting on a subway wall. I only wish that I had more time to sit on one of its grizzled benches, listening to the hum of life in the distance.

Children of Fox and Ashburnham Schools

Schoolchildren aged 7–8

—

THOUGHTS OF THE LITTL'UNS

—

"It's interracial and colourful. WE LOVE LONDON!" **Isabelle**

"When I look out of my window, I can see children and adults having such a wonderful time at the park. That is why I love London." **Eleanor**

"If I were a bird I would see the skyscrapers touching the soft clouds." **Rory**

"I love London because all of your dreams come true." **Markos**

"I love London because it's a safe country." **Mohammed**

"England's queen wears a heavy crown." **Marta**

"I love London because it helps endangered no longer be endangered." **Mia**

"Poets are everywhere and their writing floats in the air." **Rebecka**

"If you go to the Science Museum you will learn about bodies and bones." **Shayna**

"The London Eye is like a Ferris wheel, well it probably is a Ferris wheel." **Mohamed**

"Welcome to London." **Yousef**

"If you come to London, make sure you visit the museums." **Sara**

"You can hire a boat and float on one of the beautiful lakes." **Hayrah**

"Come and enjoy London, it will BLOW your mind." **Angie**

LISA BATTY

LOVE AFFAIR WITH LONDON

Ever since I was really small, growing up in the northern steel town of Scunthorpe, I knew that one day I'd find myself living in London. From an early age I fell in love. The place absolutely fascinated me; it was busy, fun, home to the craziest people and all the best music, theatres, restaurants, bars, sights and sounds. No one seemed to mind what you did and it was a place where "anything goes", which really appealed to me.

At this stage I only knew London from what I'd seen on television, films and in books, but when I was seven a school trip to "the Smoke" cemented my love of the place. We stayed just near the Natural History Museum and I spent four days in absolute awe of everything: riding the Tube, going to Piccadilly Circus, even the museums. The energy and buzz really got into my heart and right there and then I decided I'd have to work hard at school, get to university, then get a job in London where all of life was.

As I'd promised myself, after university in Manchester and time in Paris, aged 22 I headed straight down to London, staying on a friend's sofa until I found a job in advertising and a flat in Shepherd's Bush with a friend. I still remember those first few months – everything was new and there to discover, the cool bars in Soho and Notting Hill, shopping in Kensington High Street, the galleries, the museums, the markets and the people. I loved it so much and still do.

Simply wandering around London looking at streets, houses, buildings, discovering a new pub or bar, checking out the people or exploring the old parts and marvelling at their continued existence and history – this is one of my favourite things to do. There is always something new and surprising to discover. London changes, too: when I first arrived no one went east – now you can't move for hipsters. Almost every week there is a new pop-up or hidden gem to discover, sitting comfortably alongside the old stalwarts and ageing architecture from Dickens's era.

Soho, Notting Hill, Clerkenwell and Waterloo Bridge are probably my favourite areas. I've lived all over the city but now that I'm in my (early!) 40s I live with my husband in Richmond. It's beautiful, you've got the feel of the countryside, yet it's only 20 minutes on the train into Waterloo. The river here is majestic, the pubs are quaint and plentiful, and you can watch cricket on the green and keep an eye out for Mick Jagger, who is apparently a fellow Richmond-ite!

My love affair with London will never end.

MARKETING DIRECTOR AT **TIME INC.**

Mark Baxter

Camberwell gent

"RAG A BONE A' LUMBER!"

Granddad Stan was a totter in the years before the Second World War. In his mid-20s, a big, strong young man who would ride from street to street on his horse and cart doing his daily rounds in Southeast London, barking that one-time all-too-familiar cry, on the lookout for what he could pick up and then sell on.

Never fussy. Metal, old clothes, planks of timber – all considered, absolutely anything that could be re-used in those hard, hard days.

The original recycler, ahead of his time.

After being demobbed, he found he had lost his round. Someone had nipped in, when he was away fighting and later recovering from wounds picked up in Arnhem. Nice of them.

He had four kids by then, so put a shift in wherever he could, placing food on the table by simple honest graft. He also kept his hand in trawling the old street markets, seeing what was about, buying and selling.

I came along in 1962, the first son of his eldest daughter, and by the time I was ten, him a widower by then, I often accompanied him on those later trips to debris-strewn wastelands. He would pick me up early; on a Sunday he was due to come to my Mum and Dad's for a welcome roast dinner.

The drive from Camberwell, from where I rarely ventured at that young age, taking us over London Bridge and into the City, was simply magical for me: the grey swathe of river running under us, imposing concrete buildings towering above either side. It felt like we were entering a secret world. I was full of wonder.

Often our destination was Brick Lane. More precisely, the bric-a-brac market that sprung up around that area in a disorderly, ramshackle fashion on the first day of the week.

Old bed sheets placed on the pavements, displaying a seller's odds and sods, cheek by jowl with a proper market stall, with bona-fide "Anti–Que's", as I once heard them memorably described.

Stolen bikes, sparrows painted yellow to pass off as canaries, and "tomfoolery" of every shade of gold on offer. It took a wise head to get a bargain and I was soon instructed in those ways.

Breakfast first, though. A bowl of jellied eels and a cup of hot watery tea, and then somehow finding your way in and out of the maze of back streets that made up that morning's playground.

Rough, tough characters met, too. Like Mark, a bull of a man with just a couple of teeth, who smiled non-stop. Not his name, it turned out, but known as that because he made a "mark" on goods he fancied. Chalk applied to denote what he had purchased and then often sold on, before he had even laid any money down.

Granddad Stan bought and he sold and I watched and I learned. An education I would never get at school.

With time running fast and a roasted chicken waiting for us in SE5, I'd suddenly hear a shout of "C'mon son. Your Mum will kill me if we spoil her dinner" and we'd be off back to the Deep South.

I loved it then, and love it still. Like London itself, it's in my genes.

Stephen Bayley

Cultural commentator, author and critic

BATTERSEA PARK AT DUSK

South Central London has a curious character. When he was at the Post Office in the mid-19th century, the novelist Anthony Trollope despised it so much that he abolished South London postal district. S1 simply does not exist. Except, that is, as a state of mind.

Now that the badlands along the nasty, busy rut of Nine Elms Lane are being translated into London's new diplomatic quarter, Battersea Park assumes a different character. It's now more than ever a haven.

Once Battersea was most famous for the Dogs' Home; forces of inclusion recently made it a Cats' Home too. Soon, forces of real estate will make it the Battersea US Diplomats' home as well. My advice to bewildered State Department staff transplanted south of the river is to get familiar with Battersea Park. Especially at dusk.

Start at the wonderfully strange Buddhist Temple, created by the Japanese religious movement Nipponzan Myohoji in 1985. It is extravagantly kitsch and wonderfully serene, an entirely appropriate addition to a Victorian park which, during the 1951 Festival of Britain, was home to cartoonist Rowland Emett's whimsical Far Tottering and Oyster Creek Railway.

As you contemplate the gilt Buddha, ghosts of 1951 swirl around. On a good day, the staff remember to turn on the fountains in what remains of the Festival Gardens. So here you can experience a magical blend of elegy, nostalgia and religious uplift.

Even better than the ghosts is the prospect across the river on the Thames's north shore. It's an evocative view of Cheyne Walk, whose grand red-brick houses are Britain's greatest contribution to the history of world architecture: magnificent, with neither predecessors nor successors. Their red brick glows magically in the setting sun.

But this is also J M W Turner's more diffuse Thames: looking west towards the north side of Battersea Bridge you see the house where Britain's greatest painter lived, "miserable in every respect", under the pseudonym of Puggy Booth. From here he watched the sunsets that inspired him.

Whistler and Wilde were of this riverbank too. From the Buddha you can see Tite Street across the river where the two of them lived. Nearby there was also Dante Gabriel Rossetti, busy painting his sexually potent pictures of other men's wives, whose fulminating eroticism undermines lazy notions of Victorian primness.

Whistler, however, noted the sunsets more than the women. He wrote of what he saw here: "The evening mist clothes the riverside with poetry as with a veil." The series of paintings he called his Chelsea Nocturnes responded most poetically to this vision and inspired the angry Ruskin to accuse him of "flinging a pot of paint in the public's face". Which Whistler did to very great effect.

They say the Nipponzan Myohoji sect employs a hermit monk who lives in a cave in Battersea, emerging only to adjust his wind chimes and do a little tai chi at dawn and dusk, but he has never been seen. But maybe, you reflect as you amble west towards the sugared-almond-liveried Albert Bridge, his condign presence may account for the extraordinary lack of graffiti on the shrine.

Then again, maybe he is a ghost too. There are many hereabouts.

JAMES BIRCH

RELATABLE MEMORIES OF LONDON ROARING

Growing up in Primrose Hill and opposite the old zoological gardens entrance, I would quite often be woken up in the early morning by the roar of a lion, the screech of a monkey or the call of an exotic bird (sometimes one of them would escape and land in my parents' garden, whereupon they would be rescued by some London zookeeper).

Many years later, while in a remote part of Zambia, I was forced to stay in a safari camp, as there was no other accommodation available. During the night the apes raided and screeched around the camp, but I was asleep and didn't hear them. In the morning, having breakfast in the camp, the over-excited safari guides asked, "Did you hear the noisy apes last night?" I was quite dismissive and they looked at me cynically. I replied with the most annoying thing: "I lived opposite London Zoo – have you ever heard the roar of a polar bear first thing in the morning?"

I don't necessarily like zoos or safaris, but I think London's diverse sounds contribute a great deal to this city.

The roar of a motorcycle engine, leaving Andrew's Restaurant on the Gray's Inn Road, is reiterated by the continuous roaring of motorcycles at 3, 4 or 5am. I don't find this offensive – it reassures me that life is going on in London, whatever time it may be; whereas the roar of the hand-dryer in the gentlemen's lavatory leaves me exasperated and fills me with terror.

ART CURATOR

Pauline Black

Lead singer of the ska group The Selecter, actress and author

—

THE FOUNDLING MUSEUM

—

Nowhere does the old spiritual song that begins "Sometimes I feel like a motherless child, a long way from home" ring so true as when I enter the Foundling Museum in London. It is housed in an unprepossessing 1930s brick building, on the site of the original Foundling Hospital, politely nestled into a corner of Brunswick Square. As an unwanted adopted child myself, the place always reminds me that had I been born even one generation earlier, I might well have been left there.

The Foundling Museum tells the story of the Foundling Hospital, the UK's first children's charity. After 17 years of tireless campaigning, Captain Thomas Coram was granted a Royal Charter from King George II in 1739, permitting the opening of the hospital. The first child was admitted in 1741 and the last child left for a foster family in 1954, exactly the same year as I was luckily given up for adoption.

From Peter Pan to Superman, orphaned, abandoned and adopted children have a special place in our literature, but in real life very few have a happy ending.

Inside, the museum smells of polished wood. The photos of children's uniforms and the tiny beds in their dormitories tug at the heartstrings and make you wonder how anybody could condemn children to such a fate just because of an accident of birth.

Distraught mothers were told to bring a token with them to act as an identifier for their child when they left them at the Foundling Hospital, in order to prove which child was theirs if they ever returned. Such tokens could be anything from tiny pieces of fabric to coins, playing cards, jewellery and medals. The display of these objects is the most heartbreaking. I was especially moved at the sight of a tiny pink coral necklace. My mother had left something similar for me. Apparently, few mothers ever returned.

An imposing thick red-carpeted wooden staircase lined with gold-framed portraits of the great and good of the day rises through two floors, until you reach the room housing George Frideric Handel's last will and testament. He bequeathed a copy of the original manuscript of *Messiah* to the Foundling Hospital.

The Foundling Hospital was also Britain's first public art gallery. William Hogarth, who famously chronicled the underbelly of London life in his paintings, encouraged leading artists of his day to donate work. Handel donated an organ and conducted annual benefit concerts of *Messiah* in the hospital's chapel. The museum still celebrates their vision by encouraging artists, musicians and writers, and enabling them to work with vulnerable and marginalised young people today.

But nothing sums up this emotive building as well as Tracy Emin's sculpture of a pink mitten on the railings outside the museum; a tiny lost glove, a small token of a child's presence, the one left behind. It is a perfect metaphor of loss. When you reach out to touch the mitten, that which should be real and soft is a hard brass object. A reminder that life is often hard, through no fault of our own.

LEE BOFKIN

PAINTING THE CITY

London is a symphony of ringtones, traffic and construction work. In the fleeting moments of peace you may remember that you're one among ten million souls, who came here from all over the world, speaking every language and holding all manner of beliefs.

London is proof that peaceful co-existence is more than possible; it's beautiful. Its reward is the knowledge that the things that unite us are far stronger than the things that divide us.

When Global Street Art started painting we felt that Londoners wanted to live in a painted city and we knew that London's gifted and hard-working artist community wanted to paint. We began to ask landlords if our friends could paint their walls and their shop shutters. After a few cautious rejections one landlord said yes.

So we painted.

Then his neighbour said yes, and so on. A few years on, we have organised over a thousand murals. The fact that so much has been achieved with almost no funding is a testament to London's collective drive to live in a colourful city: a lot of Londoners said yes.

Grey streets are a blip for a species as colourful as ours. Today we have the organisation and drive to let grey take its rightful place amid a full palette of colours.

In future London will be awash with the colour that reflects the diversity of the people who live here.

Global Street Art exists because we want to live in painted cities. We may never reach the level of colour I imagine and it likely won't be in my lifetime, but one "yes" at a time, one wall at a time, we'll colour this city.

London is already a beacon to the world; may it grow to be an even more colourful one.

HEAD OF **GLOBAL STREET ART**

SAM BOMPAS

HARRODS FOOD HALL

I've always thought my tongue was too big for my head, and this concern may well have contributed to my taste fixation.

Over the last six years I've been working with my business partner Harry Parr to explore the unusual, exotic and unctuous produce of the fields, seas and jungles. Following the lead of gourmets like Francis Buckland (the Victorian scientist and zoophage who was the first European to document the taste of Japanese sea slug), we search out rare culinary experiences.

We have yet to go as far as Buckland. He managed to provide guests to his table with guan, curassow, boiled elephant trunk, stewed mole and rhino pie. But we have managed to feed Londoners in search of novel sensations with such notable dishes as ambergris-laced cream, perfumed eggs, radiation-aged cheese and a breathable cloud of gin and tonic that you could walk inside.

If you are searching for strange flavour experiences, you have it a lot easier than Buckland. He had to broker contra deals with zoos around Britain, providing them with new knowledge in exchange for dead animals for his larder. For you it's a lot easier. You just need to visit one of the capital's department stores for a cornucopia of flavour, stimulating pleasures and magical ingredients.

This is an account of a leisurely walk I took around Harrods, my senses alert for inspiration and unusual gustatory thrills. I'd been meaning to return for some time, having heard classy reports of the store's rejuvenated toy department. It had been too long, and this was my chance to recall the old on my way to the new.

CULINARY MAESTRO AND ONE HALF OF JELLY-MAKERS **BOMPAS & PARR**

THE FOOD HALL FRUIT COUNTER –
A CORNUCOPIA OF PLEASURE

Across the globe there are between 240,000 and 500,000 plant species that bear fruit, of which 70,000–80,000 are thought to be edible and tasty. How many have you tried? My first stop is Harrods fruit counter beneath a vast grapevine chandelier.

They have piles of knobbly, ultra-exotic and pungent fruits including tamarillos, granadillas, 14 different date varietals mounded into pyramids, pitahayas, rambutans and a pineapple so magnificent that they'll charge £12.50 for a single fruit. Harrods stop short of stocking forbidden fruit such as the unnaturally smelly durian. When I ask at the counter if it's possible for them to source one I'm told that former store owner Mohamed Al-Fayed himself banned their sale years ago. The current owners have sadly yet to reinstate the king of fruits.

Regardless, much of the stock is hard to come by regularly, such as wet walnuts or the ananas – a dried jujube that looks like a date but tastes like a sugary sweet apple. I buy four cactus fruit as I've never tried them. As I head further into the depths of Harrods I pull one out and bring it to my nose to try to get a sense of what it will taste like. I quickly realise my mistake as the fruit is covered in countless tiny spines which splinter into my hands and nose: an unwelcome sensation that will taint the remainder of my exploration. I decide to look beyond the food halls for sensory thrills and head for the mighty Egyptian escalator, a significant point of note on any Harrods visit.

PEARLS AND PERFUME

Any shopping trip is potentially erotic. As your gaze sweeps across the assembled merchandise and lingers on the silks, spices and unguents from around the world there's a real thrill.

For me Harrods is at once sleazy and luxurious. Walking through the Perfume Hall reminds me of an unbelievable rumour related by an ex-employee. The rather dubious story goes that, at one point in the store's history, all the sales assistants in the Perfume Hall wearing pearls were high-class escorts. Thrusting businessmen would supposedly stalk the hall, taking note of any assistant wearing pearls who caught their eye. By noting the time of day and the perfume concession they were, allegedly, able to call a clandestine switchboard and arrange a rendezvous for later. However unlikely, this adds a frisson to the scented air. I arrive at the Egyptian escalator and can breathe freely.

EGYPTIAN ESCALATOR

Harrods has a special place for us at Bompas & Parr. One of our more successful parties was held at Harry's house with the theme "Halloween

Harrods". We turned Harry's woodchip-papered stairwell into an ersatz version of the Egyptian escalator. Several years later, that stairwell is still gold and covered in our hand-painted hieroglyphics. One guest wore nothing but the smallest Harrods bag from the store's perfume counter. It was so tight he brought a spare in case he needed the loo.

The real Egyptian escalator is a magnificent and strange spectacle. One of my favourite details is the pair of sphinxes in the basement, one of which carries Mohamed Al-Fayed's face! I believe the other has the face of the lead architect on the project. I stop to have my photo taken with the Al-Fayed-headed sphinx.

Just next to this most extraordinary of artefacts is a fossilised lump of wood proclaiming, "You are looking at 30,000,000 years." No one minds if you touch it.

I take the Egyptian escalator to the third floor in search of more food thrills and head to the newly refurbished Toy Kingdom.

HYPNOTIC TOY DEPARTMENT

Shed Design has turned the Toy Kingdom into a hypnotic plastic land. Giant red and white mushrooms with illusory patterns work as shelving units for muscle-pumped wrestling figurines, robot helicopters and magic snow that materialises in your hand as you add water.

There's also a food element, with saccharine treats aimed at the childish palate. I'm drawn to the lurid Jelly Belly Gourmet Sodas which come in a rainbow of colours: Blueberry, Crushed Pineapple, Green Apple, Very Cherry, French Vanilla, Sour Cherry, Juicy Pear, Lemon Drop, Tangerine and Strawberry Jam. Though all the colourings are natural, it's hard to imagine even Francis Buckland having such wonders to feast on. I grab a basketful and head for the exit.

Note on dress: if you go to Harrods you need to dress appropriately. They are super-strict. I saw a couple of visitors refused entry on my way in. Here's what Wikipedia has to say on the subject:

From 1989 Harrods has had a dress code policy and has turned away several people who it believed were not dressed appropriately. These included a soldier in uniform, a scout troop, a woman with a mohican hair cut, a 15 stone (95 kg) woman and FC Shakhtar Donetsk's first team for wearing tracksuits.

Though in recent years Harrods have loosened their dress code to be more accepting of contemporary trends and fashions, they will still refuse entry for athletic singlets, cycling shorts, flip flops or thong sandals, bare midriffs or even if people are excessively sweaty!

Lloyd Bradley

Music journalist and author

SOHO CLUBBING

1976 was probably the best year there was to be young, black and a Londoner. The capital basked in a heat wave, practically everybody you knew had a job, you could park pretty much where you liked and while the mainstream music business was ushering in punk and all that went with it, a vibrant black soul scene existed almost totally under the radar. Percolating since the start of the decade, it was at its peak in 1976, with a soundtrack that ran to James Brown, Kool & the Gang, Herbie Hancock, the O'Jays, Donald Byrd, Curtis Mayfield and Earth, Wind & Fire. In parallel and often crossing over with lovers' rock reggae, it ticked all the boxes for a "born here" generation establishing an identity: it was aspirational; it dripped with black consciousness; and you could show off dancing to it.

There were local outposts in areas like Wood Green, Balham and Manor Park, but, really, everything revolved around the West End – Soho in particular. Record shops like Contempo (Hanway Street), One Stop (Dean Street) and Dobell's (Charing Cross Road) stocked the US funk imports and became meeting places and information exchanges for scenesters – this was long before Internet and the chances were your mum had put a lock on the phone. Then after dark a network of clubs opened their doors.

There was a funk calendar featuring Hunters in Kensington on a Saturday night, Paddington or the West Hampstead Birds Nest on a Sunday night. Monday off, occasional trips out of town to Scamps in Hemel Hempstead on Tuesday as we were saving ourselves for Soho as the week went on. The Big Three were Crackers at the top of Dean Street on Wednesday night and Friday lunchtime; Columbo's in Carnaby Street (now the Ben Sherman shop) on Friday night; and the high point of the week, Upstairs At Ronnie Scott's in Frith Street on Thursday.

The music at all of these spots was never less than sublime, a seamless soundtrack of pumping funk and jazz/funk. Practically nothing that had seen UK release from names that would be completely alien to Radio One – Dexter Wansell... BT Express... Mandrill – while Upstairs At Ronnie's seemed to take it one stage further, ferreting out album tracks to further our funk experience. As a result, dancing was elevated to an art form, with the circuit's superstars frequently taking over the floors in good-natured but intense competition.

One of the greatest things about it as a West End scene was that we came in from all over London, so people from Finsbury Park would mingle with people from Streatham or Ealing and so on. Because it was a tight scene – maybe 200 hard-core ravers – we all knew each other, would invite different posses to our house parties and formed crosstown friendships that still endure today. I was from Hornsey, but I met my wife, who was from Stonebridge Park, Upstairs At Ronnie's, and that isn't an unusual story.

Really, though, this was just a bonus; those Soho clubs were all about the music, and through it the sense of freedom and pride it gave to a generation that has played a big part in how London is today.

Valerie Brandes

Founder of ethnically diverse publishing house Jacaranda Books

—

MEMORIES OF LONDON

—

I was born in Stoke Newington and grew up in Hackney. The London I inhabit today is a pale, orderly facsimile of what in my memory comes to me as a richly vibrant, tragically chaotic yet happy city. It feels like a stroke of the most marvellous luck to have grown up in this community of immigrants from the Caribbean, Africa, Turkey and Cyprus, Ireland and (among the white English) a solitary part-German family. Our house, which my parents owned, was situated directly across the street from the pub and at a right angle to the local synagogue. Friday night was, as you might imagine, a raucous cacophony of the sacred and the profane.

I went to St Matthias Church of England primary school. The highlight for me was Thursday morning when we would line up, making our way into the gravel-lined churchyard and then into the (to me) exotic gothic church for full service. It was "high church": crosses borne aloft by white-robed clergy, incense burning into the air making you feel magical, otherworldly. It was the priest's angelic voice singing the Eucharist, the bells heralding communion, which we all strove to attain once we turned 11. It was gorgeous hymns and bone-stirring organ playing. It was walking super-fast past the cemetery, run-outs until the summer sun set at ten o'clock, saveloy and chips out of newspaper. It was country dancing at the town hall, my sister Esther and her best friend Helen laughing at me because of the way my head went when I danced, but you couldn't tell me anything: I was in purple gingham and the night was crisp and clear, the sky above a black velvet vision and I swear I could see the stars... It was peeking behind the flaking, red wooden door of the old plaster-maker one hot summer afternoon. Unexpectedly seeing him staring straight back at us, we ran, but he called us back, proudly showing us his work. We recognised things from the ceiling in our own house with the plaster rosettes and crown moulding. He pressed two pieces of soft plaster into our hands and we went on our way. It was jumble sales and summer fetes in the vicarage garden and it was going home to chicken and green banana dumplings, Jimmy Cliff and Jim Reeves and sweet melodious voices telling ghost stories from "back home" that lifted the hairs on the back of your neck.

It was sus laws, and true Rastas, sound systems and sweating your hair out at the dark party to Dennis Brown, Freddie McGregor and Gregory Isaacs. It was PC Blakelock, Cherry Groce, Cynthia Jarrett and Winston Silcott; it was Rock against Racism and punk rockers like human birds of paradise. It was living two doors down from where Marc Bolan grew up. Buster Bloodvessel stomping down Stokey High Road, the "hessian bag brigade" that always inhabited Church Street. It was Clissold Park in the summer: ice creams and the paddling pool and the petting zoo, and red and yellow flowers everywhere.

As an adult I have been above London. Looking down on the majestic Thames as it meanders through the city mirrored by roadways and train lines. Sleek hotels, high-end restaurants where you never order the steak because who wants to be judged on how raw they eat their meat? As spectacular as this new view of the city is, for me, it's down in Hackney, in Stoke Newington, that I will always truly find London.

Vicky Butterfly

Burlesque starlet and innovative performance artiste

MY FIRST LOVE

My London is a city of night. On a canvas of darkness, the city is painted with light in broad strokes, conjuring into existence shapeshifters and impressions. It is only the light and its reflection that exist. The shadows surrounding them confirm their hyper-reality with their nothingness.

The city exists in a state of flux: at any moment a sudden shaft of light could invoke almost any conceivable delight or horror.

As the ghostly sepia of the daytime sprawl fades, impossible colours bloom like neon flowers.

I was born just about 100 metres from Soho. My father was a Soho landlord in the '60s and his and my mother's world before me had seemed so exciting and mysterious – a tantalising world of dark shadows and reflections, whispered promises of an adult world that I couldn't wait to be a part of…

Sometimes at night I could get my father to walk us back through Soho. I loved the signs, lights glistening off tarmac, the promise of a world more exciting than mine lurking behind the windows, the girls, the clubs, the smoke. I longed for the day when I could explore this adult world I only glimpsed in the overheard conversations between my parents and their friends.

As I began to tread those roads for myself, I never realised I was seeing the end of an era: the lights went out in the windows, the neon signs were switched off for the last time and many of the faces that had drawn me there vanished.

Then one day I looked about and it was all gone.

I feel a wave of sadness when I think of all those curious travellers like myself who will never know it, but then I realised that we all have our own London. For me as a child, the night-time city offered the promise of the flâneur: a place where I could become invisible and forget loneliness by becoming one with something much larger than myself.

Looking back, I am not sure that the London I was so in love with ever existed… In it, I saw all the promise of life and adulthood, and things sighted from far away are not always as they seem close to.

But for me that can be the beauty of the affair. To know that what you love might not be real but to love it anyway. I will always be in love with that idea of London. My London will always be Soho as a beautiful woman, glistening in neon sequins and wrapped in wet tarmac. My first love.

Mark Champkins

Designer and first Inventor in Residence at the Science Museum

—

LAYERS OF LONDON

—

My favourite area of London is Borough. I love it because it feels like a part of London in which everyday Londoners have lived and worked for hundreds of years as the cityscape has evolved.

Like sediment compressed to form the layers of a rock formation, the foundation and growth of the city can be uncovered in exposed patches all over Borough. From the crumbling remains of Winchester Palace near the former Clink prison, to the unconsecrated "Cross Bones" graveyard, resting place for "single women" (a euphemism for prostitutes, known locally as "Winchester Geese" because they were reportedly licensed by the Bishop of Winchester in the Middle Ages), Borough is full of glimpses of London's past.

From what I can understand living in the area, its character seems to owe much to its proximity and status as poor relation to the walled "City of London" proper. (The name Borough apparently comes from the fact that, at one point, it was the only "borough" outside the City of London.)

Its location at the southern end of London Bridge is said to have made it a stopping point for travellers unable to enter the City after the gates closed at night, and a place of entertainment for those wishing to escape the confines of the walls. As a result, to this day I think it is one of the best drinking spots in the whole of London, with a density of old and established pubs and bars second to none.

The George Inn, off Borough High Street, is a beautiful old pub, which was a coaching inn referred to in Dickens's *Little Dorrit*, and is said to have links with Shakespeare. Nearby, in Borough Market, is the Globe Tavern, above which Bridget Jones lived in the eponymous films. Walk up past Sir Francis Drake's ship the *Golden Hind* and there are plenty of nice pubs that line the south bank of the Thames. Sat in one of these pubs I was introduced to the concept of "mudlarking". Ideally after a couple of pints, if the tide is sufficiently low, it's possible to get on to the stony bank of the Thames where, among other things, you can find fragments of thousands of discarded clay tobacco pipes. Apparently some date back as far as the 16th century. It's odd to think of the lives led by the people who held these pipes in their teeth, and what the banks of the Thames would have looked like when they idly discarded their pipes into the murky water.

Borough really comes to life on Fridays and Saturdays, when the market is on. It's been recently revamped and is not the place to go for your regular shop(!), but there are bargains to be had. One perk that I discovered living ten minutes from the market was the ability to swoop in at 5pm on a Saturday to pick up, at bargain-basement prices, all the unsold cuts of meat and vegetables before the market closes for the week.

For almost a decade I lived very close to Borough High Street in a flat where, on a Saturday night, you could hear both the sound of Big Ben and the thud of bass from the Ministry of Sound. While that probably sounds terrible, in my opinion the area where those two incongruous sounds intersect is one of the best places to be in London.

Noel Clarke

Actor, screenwriter, director and comic book writer

—

WEST IS BEST

—

I was born and raised in Ladbroke Grove. That area of London is one of the most eclectic in terms of both cultures and classes, and I love that about it. Compared with other areas of London I find it really laid back. To the north of it is Golborne Road, which is near the council building where I grew up. It has a nice bohemian vibe to it. Then down to the south of that area is Kensington High Street. It's all really mixed together, which is what I like and why I stayed. I could have moved further out and owned a much bigger property, but this is where my heart lies.

My whole life has memories in this area. The Tabernacle arts centre is a place I went to a lot when I was younger, and I've been eating at the Grove Fish Bar – the chip shop in Ladbroke Grove – for 35 years. I don't feel that old, but I've been going since I was five years old and have seen it through different owners. It's good to feel that although the area has changed, some things do stay the same.

The Kensington Sports Centre has just been rebuilt – it's called the Leisure Centre now. The new building is only a couple of years old, but I used to go there swimming all the time when I was a kid, and later on became a lifeguard and personal trainer there. In fact it's where I met my wife, and the person who got me into acting as well. So it's an important place to me.

When I was a personal trainer there, because it was the only sports centre around, a lot of people came there, including celebrities like Paula Yates, Sinead O'Connor, with their children. When you're a gym instructor you kind of get to know them. I met a guy called Rikki Beadle Blair; he turned out to be a theatre director and allowed me to audition for his show even though I wasn't an actor.

West London is my favourite place – I can't imagine living anywhere else in London; I just don't feel as comfortable. My whole life has been in the area. Holland Park is another place I love – I loved playing there as a kid and now I take my kids there… It's just a special place. I remember being in awe of the peacocks when I was a child and now I'm watching my children experience the same thing: it's a full circle.

Sadie Coles

Gallerist, art dealer

GOLBORNE ROAD

Golborne Road in Ladbroke Grove is my favourite place in London: it's a model of what London has to offer, high and low, rich and poor, local and exotic. I've been going to the Portuguese patisserie, Lisboa, since I was 18 and I still go in there in the mornings and get my Galão and, if I'm feeling cheeky, my *pastéis de nata* (custard tart). The regulars remain a mixture of Portuguese-speaking locals, white middle-class media types like me, musicians and DJs, Moroccan speakers, market vendors, students… Londoners basically, in and out of that café all day. It always feels like home to me.

There's another amazing Portuguese place called Sporting, on Elkstone Road, around the corner from Golborne. It took me a few years to pluck up the courage to try it, but the smell of sardines on the outdoor grill proved irresistible. They show noisy European football games on a big screen and it is super-friendly, cheap and delicious. We have had many a raucous party there, hosted by the persuasive Paula.

On Fridays and Saturdays I pick through the market on Golborne Road, scouring the bric-a-brac laid out on the pavements for that special find. When my son was little we would buy beaten-up toy cars from a battered cardboard box that never seemed to move or be added to. Sometimes I see my friend Tim reading a second-hand book on a second-hand chair as if the market was his sitting room. On a nice day we stop at Moroccan Fish, a food stall with stripy plastic sheeting over a plastic table where you can sit and eat the most delicious Moroccan fish. Further down there is a new Austrian restaurant that serves the best schnitzel in town. Food places come and go on Golborne Road (Pizza East is a hit with the yummy-mummy crowd) but the crowded Spanish restaurant Galicia remains as reliable as Lisboa.

When I was at university, I lived in short-life housing around the north end of Ladbroke Grove, in Notting Hill Housing Trust or Octavia Trust houses. You could stay for a year before you were moved around, gratefully slumming it in these dilapidated but grand houses. At that time – the mid '80s – Ladbroke Grove was a bit like Shoreditch is now, a place where young people congregated, still Jamaican-influenced, with proper clubs like the Globe. It was dramatically gentrified as those young people grew up and many became very successful, but Golborne Road remains a textured mix with real energy and a genuine community. The Rough Trade record shop is still there – I wave at Jeannette and Geoff through the window on my way to Lisboa – as is the office of George Galloway and the specialist vintage fashion of Rellik at the far end. There is a mix of public and private housing, with the severe modernist behemoth of Trellick Tower crowning the end of Golborne Road and setting the tone. When I've been out of the country and come in from Heathrow to my little part of London, I see Trellick Tower, dream of *pastéis de nata* and know I'm home.

Dany Cotton

London's most senior female firefighter

THE CUTTY SARK

The thing I love most about London is Greenwich Borough, but in particular, the *Cutty Sark*.

I worked in Greenwich Borough as Fire Station Commander for a number of years. I particularly like the borough because it's got such diversity – history, green parks, open areas. I've loved the *Cutty Sark* since I was a child – I visited as a kid when it was very much the original old boat.

Years later, when I was the Station Commander, the *Cutty Sark* was having renovations done and it caught fire. Probably one of my worst experiences as a Commander was hearing that news. It was about 4am; I was in bed when the message arrived. I called the command and said, "Please tell me the *Cutty Sark* isn't on fire." The receiver said, "It's six pumps – so yes, it is on fire." I remember driving from my home, which was about 10 kilometres away, with this absolute feeling of dread that something I treasured so deeply was burning.

It was an electric fire caused by a vacuum cleaner left on over the weekend – it had overheated and caught fire overnight. Thankfully, we were very successful in putting it out. During the whole rebuild process that the *Cutty Sark* went through, we – the team of firefighters and the Greenwich Fire Station – all went down to the site on several occasions to look at the work in progress. I've got photos of the rebuilding stage, and then when it reopened.

They've got massive fire safety precautions now. They have mists of water that come on, if even a small fire breaks out. These are very sensitive systems, to prevent the same thing ever happening again.

We were invited to an opening ceremony when the *Cutty Sark* was ready to open to the public again; a dinner was laid on, attended by Prince Philip, who is one of the patrons. It was held underneath the ship, in the fabulously designed space beneath the hull.

I'm now the Director for Safety and Assurance for Greater London, but I still hold the *Cutty Sark* dear. It's such an iconic ship; there's just so much history there… It's the thing I'm most passionate about in London. My colleagues think that's silly, but it really is!

PETER CRAGG

SHRINKING LONDON

London is shrinking. In a few years, it will have expanded to take in Luton, Bedford, Watford and Wellingborough. But inside, it's getting smaller.

The spaces for "others" – for queers, trans, lesbos, homos and don't-knows – are quietly disappearing. The Joiners Arms, Candy Bar, the Black Cap, the George and Dragon, and the Nelson's Head are among those that have closed in the space of 18 months. With them, we've lost spaces to be ourselves, and to unpack what it means to be different. Spaces to give someone the eye across the dance floor, maybe even ask to hold their hand. Room to dress in a bacofoil bikini and belt out Alanis Morissette in the name of performative theatre. A Thursday night when you manage to convince yourself you just saw John Malkovich dancing to Mary J Blige.

Now that we're accepted, we can get married, we have Grindr and everyone acknowledges the power of the Pink Pound, maybe those spaces aren't necessary. We don't need to be out in order to be together, be safe or experiment. Even though violent crimes against LGBTQI people are on the rise, and historical art forms and creative experimentation are on the decline. Even though the spaces we could really live in, the margins we could hold hands in, are being squeezed until all that's left is a monthly club night for 200 white gay men. And if I'm complaining, try imagining what it must be like for those who still have to keep their partners hidden from their families, who have to "tone it down" at work, or who have to laugh along when their friends talk about faggots, fairies or dykes.

Our dear, departed Harvey Milk, the first openly gay elected official in America, said, "You've got to give them hope." And as London grows, we don't have to be squeezed out. A huge grassroots campaign has been successfully fought to protect the Royal Vauxhall Tavern (the UK's oldest queer pub and performance venue) and has obtained listed status to protect it from "development" plans; many other community groups are also fighting back to protect venues. The queer community contains a thousand subheadings, and we can all stand together to demand that London makes room for each and every one of us: safe, united, creative, chaotic and fair. We can stand together and demand that London has a soul as big as its borders, and gives us all the room to live our lives as loudly or as quietly as we want.

MEMBER OF **STOP THE BLOCKS**, CAMPAIGN AGAINST THE **LOSS OF COMMUNITY & PUBLIC SPACE** IN TOWER HAMLETS

EMILY CROWTHER

FOR THE LOVE OF BRIDGES

This was an easy one for me. I don't think I could quite imagine London without its many and varied bridges. Growing up I remember that the real feeling of being in London was the sighting and crossing of one of our great bridges. They're symbolic not just to our proud and historic city, but to what it stands for. Bridge: a structure built to span physical obstacles without closing the way underneath such as a body of water, valley or road.

The simple transcription has the magnitude of what a bridge provides…a gateway, a connection, a beautiful structure marking an area, making it a point of interest, and in turn linking two. Beautiful, simple and timeless because of its many possible designs. My particular favourite is Tower Bridge, which opened in 1894 – that's 122 years of history right there. That says it all, really. When I approach it (usually by car and at night) it stands strong and haunting, almost taking me back to Jack the Ripper times, as if, if you put your nose to the air, you could smell the stench of old London smog; in crossing it, your face is hit with the mist and grime that filled the streets of London back then. It holds a nostalgia you weren't even present to experience, a spirit of the past and, to this day, a strength of our future. No matter what our buildings do, these structures are signatory. Its neighbour, London Bridge, is often confused with Tower Bridge by its observers.

At night Albert Bridge brings the magic to a photographer's lens. From a distance it seems like a Christmas decoration, elegantly strewn with "fairy lights". As you come closer these dainty additions become giant light bulbs, and its grandeur becomes clear. For me, this bridge has a different feeling from Tower Bridge, a regal sense to it. Equally proud but not quite so daunting, with its lights it provides the perfect backdrop to any folk lucky enough to reside on the river or cross it. No fear of meeting a man on horseback or a guard in armour like at Tower Bridge. As I cross over it, a sense of pride and patriotism rises up in me, the corners of my mouth turn upward, bringing a smile to my face; this is my homeland, this makes me proud to be British and live in the beating heart of our country.

HAIRDRESSER

MICKY DAWG

Professional SLEAZE

—

DEPTFORD ANCHORAGE

—

I didn't give Deptford any thought until I read *The Dark Portal* by Robin Jarvis. He described one-eyed rats, timid mice and foreboding cats in a world of sewers, folklore and survival that seemed to reflect the inky texture of my seven-year-old imagination.

A decade later, me and a few pals from South London ended up at Camberwell College of Arts. We took the 176 bus there from Penge, then we would stagger out of the college bar and take the 171 to the Goldsmiths' union for horrifically cheesy nights out fuelled on vodka, Red Bull and sambuca shots.

The Goldsmiths Tavern was better, though, we soon realised. We knew it as the GMT: a rough pub with a room at the back that played Jamaican music. After it shut we would queue for the squat opposite, where we'd meet real Deptford Rats in leather jackets with chipped teeth and attitudes like human chainsaws. Someone there told me that nearby Blackheath was built on a plague burial ground, and on a dizzy night out you could feel the breath of a thousand dead people and

the poetry of bar dwellers floating on the hot London air.

The giant anchor at the top of Deptford High Street is gone now, replaced by an ASDA loading bay, but the ship that moored there and the pirates that sailed it are still in the Birds Nest pub. The hearts of the good people that gather there are what they were and what they will always be: magical, resourceful, generous rebels in second-hand sportswear, gold earrings, hand-drawn T-shirts and cheap-yet-priceless jewellery.

And so I fell in love in Deptford. I fell for everyone – crazy cats full of prose, realistic dreamers, aliens and sweet devils. And yeah, I went to art school. I formed a band and dropped out. I'm seeing the world, but I can be on a ship on a wide ocean and catch myself thinking of that pint of Guinness in Camberwell, craving that curried goat in New Cross... Still dreaming of that house party in Deptford where I learned to be myself, to question authority and say out loud with complete certainty, "Some of my best friends are Rats, and so am I."

Theo Delaney

Director and film-maker

BAPTISM OF FIRE

It was around midday on 23 September 1972 when a long-haired man emerged from a cloud of fruity-smelling smoke in a Chiswick flat and drawled, "Umm…ok…let's go." That man was my father and he was responding to the pleading of my brother Dominic and me to be taken to a "proper football match". We hurtled across London in a beat-up mini van – purchased that very week for five quid – and arrived late to discover that the only remaining space in the ground was among the visiting team's supporters.

That is how Dominic and I, aged six and five, found ourselves among the West Ham firm at White Hart Lane when Tottenham went one up through a second-half own goal. Up to that point the lid had rattled atop the simmering menace, but it suddenly became clear that a pack of home fans had infiltrated the away end and the most spectacular brawl broke out around us. Our father, jolted from hippie reverie, picked us up and just about managed to pass us over the railings into the Spurs section before any stray boots, fists or spanners connected with our little heads.

It wasn't my first time at White Hart Lane. My debut had happened a year earlier when my uncle Bonkers had taken me to see Crystal Palace get thumped 3-0. That time we'd gone in the seats with him and his mates. They drank pints of beer throughout and bought me a big white rosette with a photo of Spurs striker Martin Chivers in the middle of it. The smell of frying onions and spilt lager permeates the memory and remains football's signature scent to this day.

London boasts 12 professional football clubs, more than any other city, so football tribalism imbues its collective psyche like nowhere else. West Ham hate Chelsea who hate Spurs who hate Arsenal; the various combined detestations are many and complex and it's bottled up all week before spewing out at weekends.

You can wax lyrical about the athleticism, the balletic beauty, the finesse of the great players, but the best thing about football is the licence to act like toddlers for two hours. Screaming, lying, cheating, abusing, kicking, pinching, crying, biting and singing silly rhymes – these are the things, on and off the pitch, that we really go to football for and it's at the derby games that you'll find the highest concentration. So it stands to reason there's no better place to be a football fan than London.

Of course a lot has changed over the years. You can't stand up any more, you can't drink beer within sight of the pitch, and the price of a Premier League seat would have bought a fleet of the mini vans that took us to the game in 1972. But the fundamentals remain. It is as tribal as ever and the visceral hatred hasn't dissipated one bit, even if the cops have found a way of stemming the violence in the grounds.

The reason English football commands a global audience far bigger than any other nation's is the unique, win-at-all-costs zeal evident on the field and in the stands. And London is its zenith.

Following that exhilarating experience in 1972 I became an obsessive Spurs supporter for life. Dominic, curiously, became a West Ham nut.

Louise Dennington

Interior designer and yoga teacher

—

EAST FINCHLEY

—

When I first moved out of my parents' home I lived in Stepney Green. Since then I have lived all over, including Lancaster Gate, Angel, Stoke Newington, Fulham, Elephant and Castle, Ladbroke Grove, a quick four-year stint in India, and currently Haggerston. But home is, and always will be, East Finchley, where I grew up. East Finchley is a pocket of Barnet in North London. A friend recently tried to say that it doesn't count as London, but it very much does! It's the pockets that make London.

I love that although, yes, we are not in the thick of it, you can be somewhere like Oxford Circus in 20 minutes if you want to be – If you know the trick of taking the Northern Line Bank branch (not Charing Cross branch) and hopping onto the Victoria Line at Euston, where you only have to walk across the platform. At the same time, you can easily get to places like Ally Pally (Alexandra Palace) or Hampstead Heath and have an amazing view of our city's epic skyline, and be out of it looking into it. The hustle and bustle, and the chaos and the calm. The air is always so crisp and fresh in both those places – perfect for long walks, meditation, new perspectives. We have a family tradition of going to the Heath on Boxing Day or New Year's Day, no matter how tired or hungover we are. The workout our lungs get and the hot chocolate or tea at Kenwood House afterwards make it thoroughly worth fighting the cold and putting up with a runny nose.

We have some "claims to fame" in East Finchley, like the Phoenix Cinema which is apparently the second oldest continuously running cinema in the UK: it opened in 1912. My Mum and her two sisters worked there in their teens. Still one of my favourite and cosiest places to go to watch a movie.

I also love that East Finchley, and in particular our road, has a real sense of community, which I know some people think you don't get in London. I remember, growing up, if I'd forgotten my keys (it happened a lot!), at least a couple of neighbours had spares of ours (and vice versa), and if they weren't at home there were plenty of other doors to knock on and be welcomed in for a cup of tea and/or to watch *Neighbours* (the Aussie TV show). I've never lived anywhere since where I've known at least half the people on the street.

We have husband and wife Brian and Joy, who've lived here for over 65 years and have family who lived here before… Alan on the corner, a London "black cabbie"… Dorrie, next to us, who's from Mauritius, a lecturer at Westminster University… My parents, one from England and one from Sri Lanka, both environmental health officers (one for Kensington and Chelsea, the other for Haringey). This is a cool representation of what occurs all over London, and why it's great…a meeting ground for different and diverse people, backgrounds, histories, cultures and ideas.

Leigh Dickinson

Builder

—

STILL LONDON

—

It may be clichéd to say that London is defined by its rich socio-cultural multiplicity, that London is many things. But I was raised in a place characterised by flatness, a place where the summer yields great vistas of sun-burned yellow corn, of winding roads and paths that stretch back thousands of years, a place where the wind blasts in off the North Sea, fresh from Scandinavia, buffeting the coast so hard it cuts you through. While to you this may sound romantic, idyllic – Arcadian, even – to me, this place is thoroughly predictable, sombre and of small interest.

By contrast, London is an ever-expanding, churning mass of arid, neon-grey, commercially franchised consumerist temples clad in ornate stonework and classical friezes. It is the islands of well-managed parks and fields that punctuate the geometry of the city with the illusion of chaos. London is church spires, it is tourist attractions, palaces, towering skyscrapers walled with glass, topped with gleaming pyramids, looking down on the mess of live tenement blocks, rented homes and disused factories in which reverberate the echoes of every drama of life, played out under an unremitting, oppressive sense of age – as though history is almost living on top of the present, side by side with us as we walk the streets.

The most intimate encounters I have with London involve its past. I am a builder and so often have cause to dig, to cut into London so that a service pipe may be connected, to underpin a building or to further advance the city's expansion into the earth – when "digging down" new basement levels.

I displace the sand and gravel and brick and clay upon which London stands. The experience is characterised by toil, exertion, isolation (occasionally fulfilment), but most of all by a sense of pervading stillness, of long-static material, in among which the odd discarded thing may be incidentally encountered.

It is due to these objects or "artefacts" that I am able – even when engaged in a mundane pursuit such as digging – to maintain a dim spark of romance, a hope of finding something that might speak to me of the past's intrigues: a piece of Mediterranean pottery from the Roman era, an old coin, a Saxon king buried in his greatest warship, bedecked all about in glorious finery, heraldry and general regal effects… Even perhaps a piece of the true cross or, better still, King Henry VIII's bespoke lamb-bowel prophylactic.

Surprisingly, I have never been lucky enough to find anything so rare or ridiculous. The things I have found that speak to me of the presence of London's past are cow bones, oyster shells, little clay pipes and motor oil – seeping down slowly through the strata. Oysters dredged up from the Thames estuary, meat from beasts slaughtered at old Smithfield, pipes cooked in brick kilns on the capital's outskirts: things of little value, tossed into middens and discarded. Forgotten things that few care for, but that have allowed me to commune with an older London, with London's biology and its appetites, in a way that few are privileged to enjoy.

London, thank God for the digging man: London, thank God for the spade operator and the great "shoveler" – for we thank God for you.

Helen M Donohoe

Author; former Director of Public Policy at Action for Children

YOU WERE WAITING

You were waiting. I took tiny steps and lightly took your hand. Your thick wind churned. I had no plans. Your pavements clutched me; commotion, collisions, rebellious rush. I sensed freedom but seizure in your grit and your dust.

Then tight. You held me. Nights merged with days. You pushed me. I fell forwards, through the glittering haze. You wooed, I blushed. I denied you. I hid. I ran. But you waited, with tolerance, as you have always done.

I had to be brave. Your colours, your speedy rush over your ancient cellars. Your antique cobblestones, coating your history beneath, and your glass-fronted towers with their cloud-bursting reach.

A delirious drunkard was born in me then, bursting with energy, eyes wide open. My brain buzzed by your reckless city whirl. How could you – *mo chroí** – do such things to this girl?

Then I tripped. I grazed my knuckles like beginners often do. From down on my scarred knees I looked up to you. Your troubles looked back, and your danger and your power. London. You could go from awe to awry in less than an hour.

My bag was nearly packed.

But you pulled me back.

Time allowed growth and we grew along together. I surveyed your pubs: Victorian décor to caged-up windows, Arsenal fanatics, ear-crushing music, Irish singers, city slickers, gardens made from concrete corners, gay men in leather chaps, women cultivating their tufts of 'tash. And quiet

corners and pints of Guinness and open fires, occasionally not a peep for almost five minutes.

Then your parks I frequented, with picnics and blankets, shared with drunks and the middle-class demented. I took time to visit the monuments to the legends in your soil. You showed me scuffles and chattering classes and psychotic street poets. Buildings of stone, brick and marble. Cold, sharp, glass. Never dark. Rat race. Happy face. Sad face. Crammed into the tiniest space.

As I aged, my ears adjusted. The chirp of little green birds, and cricket matches and more than your screaming I heard your calm hushed words. You were modest and proud, quiet and loud. You felt like home. A dream of my own.

And so we settled. You gave me greenery and I gave you flowers. When you gave me a rooftop, I sat and read and pondered and slept and watched you for hours.

You gave me a wife and children and what I never imagined I would have in my life. A house, our house, in the middle of our street.

Yet every day is different. And, London, as a love affair you are never over and never complete. I see pubs turned into mosques down unfamiliar streets, florists' shops watched over by smiling squat bulldogs. I've still so many hills, pastures and alleys I want to see. So many of your benches, dedicated to former lovers, on which I want to fall asleep.

* *my heart* in Gaelic

Alex Eagle

Designer and shop owner

—

SHOPPING IN LONDON

—

I'm biased, but I think London has some of the best shopping in the world. Clarendon Cross in Notting Hill, Kinnerton Street, St James's, Marylebone High Street, Pimlico – all beautiful retail oases filled with unusual shops and good restaurants.

So much of it is about heritage. Of course Londoners aren't the only city dwellers with heritage, but the thing here is that British style walks a wonderful line between tradition and eccentricity. You can buy pieces that have been made the same way for centuries, from people who know everything about what they are selling, in stores that inspire you to think creatively about what you want to wear, sit on or look at.

All my favourite stores have an inspiring person at their heart. I have been going to Egg on Kinnerton Street since I was a teenager. Maureen Doherty's serene enclave of unusual, luxurious brands has filled my wardrobe as well as being a huge influence on how I create my own retail spaces. The same with the Society Club – the owner, Babette, is crazy about books and cocktails, so she's created a private members' club on a tiny street in Soho with shelves rammed full of first editions and beautiful coffee-table books, and a brilliant cocktail maker mixing Old Fashioneds. Babette is so enthusiastic and knowledgeable, you always leave having gained much more than a book.

When you go shopping, you want to feel as if you are going somewhere you will find the thing that you need, but without being completely overwhelmed. It takes so much energy to edit things, but the best shops in London are those that have done the edit for you, where you are going to have a wonderful experience while spending your money. If you buy a hat from Lock Hatters on St James's Street, you are buying into more than three centuries of expertise. When you go to Howe in Pimlico, you are walking into Chris Howe's personal visual universe, filled with antiques and handmade furniture and design ware that he's sourced himself. It's so fun, going to these places. There's a security of style – the taste is assured, the people who work there know the products inside out, they know exactly what will suit you, it's bespoke. It's about refinement. Chris Howe can talk about a sofa for two hours so that, when you buy it, you know why. Maureen knows her customers at Egg. Babette knows books. You get an education, depth, and everything has worth. It's shopping that results in you acquiring fewer things, but understanding them more. That's what I've tried to do with my own space, Alex Eagle on Lexington Street. I have hand-picked everything, investigated the provenance of the furniture, talked to the designers of the clothes – there is a reason why everything is in the edit, and I hope that shows.

And because you're in London, all these shops are in the loveliest places filled with the best restaurants – if you've been in St James's, you can fall straight into Wiltons. Kinnerton Street has a lovely pub, Clarendon Cross has Julie's, Pimlico has La Poule au Pot, Lexington Street has Andrew Edmunds, Marylebone has La Fromagerie. Shopping should be a pleasure, and you get that joy in the best London shops.

Travis Elborough

Writer and cultural commentator

A LITTLE OF LONDON MAGIC

In these present times and with so much of the London I've known and loved over the last 30 years or so either lost or disappearing or under threat, it can feel as though a little of the old magic of the place has gone. It is hard, after all, not to experience change as loss. Especially when those changes so often mean that much-cherished haunts vanish to be superseded by clone chains or are converted into luxury flats (and a home in London is rapidly becoming a luxury few can afford in itself) and familiar streetscapes and buildings are eradicated or rendered invisible by new additions. But actually it is sometimes a wonder how much of the old capital remains, seemingly impervious to the shifts in social mores, let alone the arrival of social media.

And whenever I feel the need to reassure myself about the wonder of the capital I head to one of its greatest, if perhaps its most idiosyncratic, independent shops: International Magic in Clerkenwell.

For anyone who has ever wondered quite where in London they might be able to obtain a wand that turns into a bunch of flowers or a set of steel rings that defy the normal laws of physics by slotting in and out of one another, then this is the emporium for you.

Even if you haven't, go anyway, it is a kind of tiny Wunderkammer of all things magical – and that's definitely magical with a "c" rather than your Aleister Crowley-Anton-LaVey hexes and sex with goats stuff with a "k".

If you somehow still fail to be impressed by the selection of tricks, the collection of photographs on the shop's walls of heavily eye-linered prestidigitators of yesteryear coaxing doves from thin air or rabbits from hats offers a spectacle not seen in any mainstream gallery or museum.

International Magic was founded by the magician Ron MacMillan over 50 years ago (a shot of Ron, resplendent in white tie and dinner jacket, has pride of place in the store) and was run for many years by his widow, Teresa. The shop's name derives from the fact that in the 1950s Macmillan was in a double act with the legendary Ali Bongo; the pair performed a language-barrier-breaking silent show that was extremely popular in Germany.

BEN ELLIOT

MOUNT STREET GARDENS

There is a place in London that is important to me, and important for a number of reasons: a square in Mayfair called Mount Street Gardens. It's played a role in my life at various ages. It has a school in it, and a church, so there's always a thoroughfare of different people passing through, or having picnics in it, or just passing time there.

The reason why, emotionally and spiritually, it is important to me is my grandfather, who fought in World War II. He was a very modest war hero, as most people who fought in that war were or are. He received two MCs. He wasn't a businessman, but in the late 1940s, early 1950s, he opened what would probably be called a gentlemen's wine business. There wasn't international trade at that time; the only people buying expensive wine post-war were Oxbridge colleges. My grandfather spent most of his time speaking to the dons from those institutions.

His office was based near where Harry's Bar is today, around the corner from Mount Street Gardens. I remember him telling me he used to go and read a newspaper there – he used to tell my cousins and me stories about it. I'd imagine him sitting on a bench, rather elegantly – more elegantly than I – pondering life, in the 1950s and '60s. So when I moved to London and my first job was working in the kitchens of Harry's Bar, I used to go and sit there in my chef's whites (I was a terrible chef but couldn't get another job). I'd go and smoke a cigarette in the square.

Since then I've continued to visit some of the buildings on the square. Some are quite Victorian, but the light in it is good, particularly in the afternoon, and I've found it to be something of a refuge. It's a place I go to get away from the hustle and bustle of London; it's a place I've spent time thinking about things.

I like Mayfair enormously: it's an arterial route for my offices. I have a lot of commercial and business interests in Mayfair, but I prefer sitting in Mount Street Gardens to Berkeley Square, which is at the heart of Mayfair. It's the place I always come back to, partly because of my grandfather's connection to it, but also because it holds memories from when I first came to London aged 18. Now, 23 years later, it is still my favourite spot.

CO-FOUNDER OF
QUINTESSENTIALLY LIFESTYLE GROUP

Suzette Field

Author and event organiser; Founder of The Last Tuesday Society

—

BROMPTON CEMETERY

—

We frequently hear stories of oligarchs and other shady foreign businessmen buying up property in Chelsea in order to "park" their black-market money: a practice that has led to whole streets of multi-million-pound mansions in the Royal Borough being left dark all year round. Yet there is one area of Kensington and Chelsea which in my opinion is all the better for being entirely and permanently uninhabited by a single living soul. I'm talking about my favourite spot in London: Brompton Cemetery. Apart from the fortnightly 90-minute vocal interruption from the 43,000 fans at neighbouring Stamford Bridge football stadium, which is met with stony silence from the 205,000 subterranean residents of the graveyard, this 15-hectare swathe of Central London is a permanent oasis of stillness and peace. As a writer, I often repair here when I'm seeking out silence and solitude to contemplate some new project.

Brompton Cemetery was one of the "Magnificent Seven" cemeteries built in Victorian times to soak up the demand from the city's overflowing burial grounds. I love the unkempt wildness of the place: so different to the elegantly manicured memorial parks in California, where I grew up. When I moved to London as a schoolgirl it conjured up images in my teenage mind of Cathy and Heathcliff and the graveyard in Gimmerton chapel.

Writers before me have gathered inspiration from Brompton's 35,000 tombstones and mausoleums and their accompanying stories. H G Wells was fascinated by the legend that the mausoleum of the Courtoy family – a 6-metre tall trapezoid of dark polished granite with a pyramidal roof and a huge copper door – secretly houses a time machine. The monument was designed by the eccentric Victorian inventor Samuel Warner with sculptor Joseph Bonomi and bears mysterious inscriptions based on Egyptian hieroglyphics and some of Leonardo da Vinci's more obscure sketches. These allegedly contain the secret of time travel. Warner was murdered in mysterious circumstances and shortly afterwards the key to the mausoleum's great bronze door went missing. To the frustration of Wells and other investigators, the lock has proved impervious to even the most skilled locksmiths. Wells based his story "The Time Machine" on the legend.

A little more prosaically, Chelsea resident Beatrix Potter was a frequent visitor to the cemetery for 50 years and it seems borrowed the names of many of her woodland characters from inscriptions on the headstones (deceased locals include a Peter Rabbett, a Jeremiah Fisher, a Mr Nutkins, a Mr Brock and a Mr McGregor).

Over recent years I've become involved with the cemetery and now host regular fund-raising events there. "London Month of the Dead" – a festival devoted to the celebration of mortality which I co-curate with events organisers Antique Beat – takes place each October and features talks, candlelit concerts, ghost stories and seances in the cemetery. In promoting awareness of Brompton I'm hopefully helping to bring Londoners into contact with their past and, inevitably, their future.

Stephen Fry

Comedian, actor, writer and TV presenter

LONDON LIKE THE ENGLISH LANGUAGE

I'll tell you what it is about London. And I'll tell you in English, because whenever I think of the English language I think of London and whenever I think of London I think of the English language. And I love them both with all my heart and soul. And perhaps for the same reasons. You be the judge.

We open our mouth to speak English and a stream of varied discourses is released. Commercial, piratical, Shakespearean, jazz, biblical, aristocratic, American, criminal, Miltonian, convict, gangster, gangsta, Australian, Compton and Cambridge…all of them jostle in the same sentence and none takes priority.

No anglophone equivalent of the Académie française exists to control, regulate, stipulate, prescribe and proscribe the English language.

And look at London's architecture: Elizabethan, ecclesiastical, corporate, Victorian, domestic, artisan, retail, Georgian, modernist and medieval, vulgar and refined, all higgledy-piggledy and hugger-mugger.

No planner fenced off one part of London from another, herded it into a museum city.

I don't wish to insult the French language or to impugn Paris. But let's be honest, attempts to herd and control either the language or the city do not have happy outcomes.

The coexistence in London of the crass, corporate and commercial with the refined, religious and royal makes for a great vibrant and throbbingly, jerkingly, frothingly exciting clash.

And it was the Clash after all who wrote "London Calling…"

Steve Furst

Comedian, actor and writer

—

FROM THE DESK OF LENNY BEIGE

—

1995; the century was coming to a close and Britpop was about to explode and make London swing once again. But there was already an underground revival movement that was being talked about: easy listening. Club Indigo was a regular fixture at the legendary Madame JoJo's and we followed soon after. No. 3 New Burlington Street was a small venue off Regent Street which, over ten weeks, we had packed with a small but fanatical following for our cabaret featuring freaks, piss-poor variety acts and almost inedible food with a no-riffraff guarantee.

We needed to expand. And quickly.

I had heard about a venue that was only used for a cabaret aimed squarely at bewildered tourists, bussed in on a package tour. With their resistance already weakened by jet lag and finally done in by almost undrinkable wine-style drinks and overpriced spirits, they sat and watched musical-theatre graduates present a half-arsed tribute to London musicals. It lasted 90 minutes and was eminently forgettable. The good news that it only ran for five nights of the week. My brother Sammy and I decided to set up a meeting.

The Talk of London was located in the New London Theatre building, where *Cats* had been running since about 1848. The Talk was on the first floor and the main theatre was above that. We were due to meet with Rae MacIntyre, the manager, at lunchtime on a Monday. When I entered through the double doors into the venue I can safely say my life changed. I looked

at the room, realised it was the greatest cabaret venue in London and knew it was to be our home. We wanted a Friday night but we were offered a Sunday. Sunday would do. Eventually we made Wednesday our regular night.

What made this venue so unique was the fact that it was round, affording all punters a perfect view of the stage. It was on three levels, but only imperceptibly so. The dance floor in the middle of the room was classic parquet and the stage was the *pièce de résistance*. The sheer curtain around the curved raised dais opened. Then, at the touch of a button (located on the back wall), an extra part of the stage hydraulically emerged from under the main stage, creating a thrust/walkway. Rae told us, "We never use that feature."

As soon as he said those words I realised Rae was an idiot. That feature was to be my signature start to shows that we hosted in the venue for over five years. Not only that, we recorded 16 TV shows there, too. I did countless TV and radio interviews in that venue and knew ever nook and cranny intimately.

The backstage was a disgrace, but it became our disgrace for the nights we were there. A confusing warren of rooms housed the waiters' lockers, the almost defunct showers and changing facilities that would have shamed a 1950s Romanian gymnasium.

But that main show room was almost as much of a star as me. A room fully carpeted with easy-stack banqueting chairs around individual tables in a room redolent of a 1970s

cruise liner was a thing of beauty. People would dress appropriately in shirts, ties, suits, gowns, sexy evening wear…it was the best-dressed room in town. Those were the greatest nights of my life. It was more than just a cabaret show with big-name attractions like Robbie Williams, Sacha Baron Cohen, Chas & Dave, Matt Lucas and so on…it was a way of life.

After we finished in 2001 and we'd presented our final show, I never thought we would be there again. Especially when it changed management and became Guanabara,

a Brazilian nightspot. Then two years ago I found myself back on the same stage (sadly minus the hydraulic appendage) introducing some of our favourite acts to the gathered faithful. Almost 20 years had passed. Sure, they had removed the carpet, put in benches, spruced up the bar area and apparently never cleaned backstage, but that room still had the magic. And we are back there twice a year to honour the space in the way it should be honoured: with the greatest cabaret show in the world.

Luke Gamble

Financier and entrepreneur

A CONVERSATION WITH THE KING

To me London has been many things in my life, not least a best friend and lover. As we seem to know in this life, you love, you hate, you cry, you lust and you fight, but above all you love. This love brushed against me first when I was a little'un just a frisbee's throw from Clapham Common and the jovial Irish influence, but it struck with full force during my last year at university, my last summer before leaving and coming back to town, trying to grow up (whatever that means). The phone went, and that random call led to the best summer of my life. As I was looking for a permanent idea of myself in the world, London took me in again, as it has so many, and found me a home: Ranston Street, NW1, next to Lisson Grove, and boy I loved it. A fairly underappreciated part of the capital in many ways, it has a few great galleries, the local hum of the shisha pipe, and a damn good kebab if you know where to look. It's not that far from a day's cricket at Lord's, with Little Venice over the way and the wonderful stucco terraces of John Nash's Regent's Park.

For ever etched into my mind: the day I moved into Ranston Street for the summer, meeting my flatmates (very lucky to be living with four girls, thanks to the man or woman upstairs). Off we trotted round the corner, an extremely attractive blonde and I, and my eyes dropped into my heart. We rounded the bend and we bumped into one of those A-grade London scenes, pub people sipping and slipping out onto the street as if a church service had just ended, a busker's folky tones drifting among it all. There we sat, enjoying the brain-altering taste of the rightly famous Lisson

Grove fish and chips on our laps with a cold beer to share on a beautifully balmy London summer's eve – we wanted for nothing. We found ourselves that day in more ways than one. Our journey took us up to Primrose Hill, where the same scene was unfolding at the Queen's, a gem of a pub that knows its script, situated at the end of Chalk Farm Road. It serves to grease the wheels of tourists, the gentrified and many a Londoner alike. Looking from the hill, we were able to soak up the vast metropolis, with St Paul's always standing tall in glorious juxtaposition. Heading into Soho, late into the small hours, Mad Hatters knowing White Rabbit was on his way, we felt our hearts in our hands and in the heart of it all, whipping in and out of the caverns and alleys which pipe the blood around this concrete body. When this city gets as hot as it did that night, something changes, people change, some would say, for in those moments all the elements that make life what it is seem to hold still, in freeze-framed celebration. It liberates all, moves you, engenders the smile, shakes the hips. It creates fellowship in this city.

For all its wonder, you do hate it sometimes, like anything, so the indelible memories of those liberated moments become all the more precious.

That night was perfection, it hit me right between my eyes and its scar I wear with pride. London was buzzing, the heady madness in all its beauty. The city captured me and made me feel it was possible, all possible: and that moment I will never forget as long as I live. The sense of being and the endless stories that will never stop being written were all there suddenly in my

heart…all discovered here…and my love affair had begun to be written. That night was the first real conversation I had with this city, and once you find that dialogue, that sense of it, you are hooked like no other place I have ever been. It is that déjà vu of a future flashback that I love, the familiar yet the unknown tales to come each time.

For me, the sense of what London is combines all these elements, making you realise what a fabulous friend you are speaking to. Like us all, beautiful, difficult sods with humanity in our hearts, this city provides us with the privilege to be in this story and play our part, for good and for bad. London, I love you.

GRANT GILLESPIE

BOHO IN SOHO

I first visited the dirty beating heart of Soho when I was a student and I felt as if I'd come home. I watched the squalid beauties, the artistic idlers and the eloquent drunks stagger along Old Compton Street and knew I wanted to be just like them. Cut to ten years later, when I began living my dream, and I've been a happy Soho somnambulist ever since.

To my mind, Soho is the embodiment of all that's boho: a nocturnal playground peopled by artists, prostitutes and vagabonds. It's a place for lovers and the unloved; the creatively rich and the morally bankrupt; a jewel in a drunken drag queen's crown. It's the square mile of anything goes and I remember hearing a conversation between a Walker's Court pimp and a punter that I think captures Soho's spirit of experiment…

Pimp (in a London accent that would make Dickens proud): "What you looking for, mate? Ladies? Men?"

Oversized American tourist: "Gals, definitely gals! Oh, wait…hang on a minute… I could get with a guy?"

Pimp: "Whatever you want, mate. Your call."

Oversized American: "No, no… I'll go with a gal for today."

All life passes below my window or passes out here, and I relish the motley parade. There's the Indian gentleman in his jaded Savile Row suit and Eton hair, losing a row with himself; the Brazilian transsexual crack whore with breasts to die for; the old lady with a crescent-moon spine clutching her threadbare bespectacled bear; the perpetually jaunty whistling man with his silver-topped cane; and the ungainly hen-party gals trying to sashay in sashes.

Soho also has its ghosts. An elderly actor friend of mine recalls running naked through Soho with Allen Ginsberg shouting, "*Nous sommes des anges!*" ["We are angels!"] and I'm certain that deceased Soho icons Sebastian Horsley, Paul Raymond, Jeffrey Bernard, Muriel Belcher and Francis Bacon will be revolving in their graves about all the demolition and redevelopment of their erstwhile parish.

There's no disputing that Soho is changing, and probably not for the better, but there are still a few gems left, notably the French House pub, Ronnie Scott's and Bar Italia. And there are some fabulous new venues that do the area proud: the Society Club and Lights of Soho. Besides, Soho will forget. It's a willing amnesiac: every evening it turns into a raving, deliriously happy drunk and every day it wakes with a well-earned hangover and no idea what happened the night before…

ACTOR, NOVELIST, SCREENWRITER
AND **PARISH OF SOHO** RESIDENT

IVO GORMLEY

BOW LOCKS

I arrive at Bow Creek along Limehouse Cut, a straight slice through London from St Katharine Docks to the River Lea. By the time I arrive I'm fully into my run.

Bow Locks are a series of mechanical locks that connect the tidal water of Bow Creek to the canal system. As soon as you pass under the A12 you're aware that you're leaving inhabited residential London.

It's a gap in the city, the infrastructure for controlling nature; the locks, the bridges, the canals are the dominant features of the landscape and are the only route you can follow. You are very aware of feeling like an outsider as a human being.

This space, the floating island of locks between two rivers, one tidal and one controlled, makes me think about London as a tidal plane with the Thames shifting course, before it had buildings on it.

If you look up you can see and feel how London turned from that time to this, and how its epochs now live together.

Bow Creek runs into the Thames in the middle of the Roman-initiated Port of London. Now shipping continues in its contemporary form – you pass an Amazon warehouse on your right.

Many of our resources have passed through here and still do – the rail bridge carries freight over your head, the road services the industrial park containing the eight remaining gas towers to your right. The canals which the trains and cars have superseded are now a silent route into the heart of this changing space that will continue to be reinvented. The place has all the things that keep the city running, but is at the same time a relief from the city.

When I hit the bridge it's the middle of my run. I'm feeling a strange kind of elation and quiet that only releases with the outburst of effort at running up the steep ramp of the footbridge. Hitting the top of the bridge, you're up high, in between two rivers, in a gap in London, at peace.

Coming down from the bridge, senses are heightened, it's raining and wisps of canal boats' wood smoke drift across the footpath as you head north and back to where people live.

FOUNDER OF **GOODGYM**, WHICH HELPS
YOU TO **GET FIT BY DOING GOOD**

Olivia Grant

Actress

THE CHELSEA PHYSIC GARDEN

There are a lot of reasons why I love the Chelsea Physic Garden. One of them is that London is a city of hustle, anonymity and intrinsic freneticism – a more mature cousin of New York perhaps – and there's something calming about sitting in a walled garden in the middle of it all.

It is bizarrely removed even from the hum of Chelsea, despite sitting at its heart. In fact, the whole area around the Chelsea Pensioners' building – Swan Street, Tite Street and the rather dreamily named Clover Mews where I was lucky enough to live for a year – has an other-worldliness. The pastel-coloured houses don't come up for sale, no one ever seems to work, and the extent of the local activity is the odd resident pottering around in loafers with no socks and a newspaper tucked under their arm.

The Physic Garden was established as an Apothecaries' Garden back in 1673. The second-oldest botanical garden in Britain evidently holds thousands of useful, edible and, most importantly, medicinal plants. Not that I've spent a huge amount of time studying or sampling. It's good to know that such plants are there, though, growing quietly among the rock gardens. Ready to be put in a pestle and mortar and have an apothecary do to them…well…whatever vaguely magical things apothecaries do.

The garden itself is not big at all. It only takes a short time to wander round it. There's a café inside the house which sits inside the walled grounds – it's a simple café, but it does an excellent cream tea, which is one of my many weaknesses. A very happy spring afternoon would consist of slowly eroding a slice of Victoria sponge and spending time under the garden's awnings, reading E M Forster novels and quietly pretending I am in a Merchant Ivory film.

There was another time, when the Physic Garden was undergoing renovations, that saw me squeeze through the railings with a boy… I may be wrong but I feel the ancient apothecaries would approve. For if real Londoners didn't kiss in walled botanical gardens under the cover of darkness, then Richard Curtis wouldn't have been able to pen the line "Whoops-a-daisy" in *Notting Hill* and we'd all be much the poorer. That's my reasoning, anyway.

I urge you to go before it becomes the Wolseley – which does excellent Battenberg cake on a Thursday, by the way – and the Chelsea Physic Garden is suddenly on every tourist's list. For now, at least, it remains a quintessentially English haven; somehow outside of time.

Lucy Granville

Urban cyclist

—

MY LONDON CYCLING STORY

—

I bought my current bike 15 years ago. It was chained to a lamppost outside a grocer's on Exmouth Market in London with a for-sale note tied to it. I asked the very old and spritely man who worked for the Sikh owners at the shop about it. He had been in prison in Australia for many years, he wanted me to know. He was full of life, as if they had given it to him. He was selling the bike for £20. I was thrilled, as it was a fine bike.

I had no idea about the make or anything, but it wasn't too heavy and didn't seem to have any cracks in the frame. It turned out to be a Coventry Eagle, probably an early 1980s model, judging by the safety mark. It's a remarkably good bike. I have never had any problems with it, despite constantly and mercilessly thrashing it along the pitted city streets.

When I was a pre-schooler in the late 1970s, Dad used to give me a lift to nursery on the back of his bike, on his way to work in the City. He wore his suit. No changing in and out of cycling clothing for him. I don't recall any urban cyclists doing that in those days. One or two still even wore bowler hats. Before we set off, Dad would carefully fold his suit-trouser legs at the ankle, put his metal bike clips on, and that was that. Good to go.

There were barely any other cyclists on the roads. There wasn't a bike culture back then. The huge drifts of cyclist drones in heavily branded Lycra, hi-vis, tech-protected eyes and backpacks, silently massing at red lights, are a recent phenomenon.

My child seat was a tiny wooden chair in an iron frame with little narrow armrests. I don't remember any straps. I don't remember wearing a hat. We'd fly across the wide downhill right-hand turn southwest onto St John Street, just past Angel, man and baby both leaning into the corner.

I rode everywhere I went from about 13 or 14. From 16 I cycled to my sixth-form centre every day, up Holloway Road from the Highbury end. Once I wasn't paying attention and was stopped by a fridge-freezer someone had left in the road.

Many people, in particular other women, say to me, "How can you cycle? It's so dangerous in London! I wouldn't dare! I'm no good at cycling! How can you cycle home late at night? That's so dangerous!" I really don't understand this attitude. I always feel powerful and strong when I ride. I get an adrenalin and confidence buzz when I successfully take calculated risks, which is every few seconds if you ride in an urban environment crowded with other operators. Most of the elements you are in play with are engine-powered machines, lots of them, and the playing field is a highly dynamic and densely control-featured road system.

These empowered feelings are a contrast to what I endured being on foot as a young girl,

in school uniform a lot of the time, of course. Men would often stare at me, which made me feel intensely uncomfortable. They made comments about my skinny, awkward, tall, long-legged body. They would banter with me, although I had no idea how to respond. I was jolted out of my thoughts by being told to cheer up, or by wolf whistles from invisible heights of scaffolding. Or by whispered, barely audible filth in my ear, or suggestive remarks out of the windows of cars slowed down to cruise along at my speed, as I attempted to walk "unselfconsciously" along the street.

Sometimes, I knocked on strangers' doors on my way home from school, pretending I lived there, to shake off men I thought might be following me, especially in winter, when I walked home in the dark. It wasn't as stressful as it sounds. It was just normal. Life was a bit like a computer game, dodging jeopardy, adrenalin rush, beating heart, normal again.

It was not particularly worth mentioning to anyone. In any case, all the adults around me could observe it for themselves, and no one ever said anything, so why should I?

We had self-protection advice at school. "Pick your nose when you are on public transport, to make yourself seem unappealing." The only suggestion I liked was holding one of your keys between your fingers so you could stab someone in the eye if they attacked you.

I wasn't too bothered at the time. It's only now, thinking about it, that I realise my bike got me off the streets.

As I got older, cycling London continued to have great benefits. On chilly mornings in the office, after battling through the cold, others might be bleary-eyed at their desks, clutching cups of tea, while I sat down invigorated. I wanted to kiss the sky! Serotonin is a powerful drug. Working in the City in a giant investment bank, I found my bike would catapult me out of the nightmarish traffic gridlock every day. I would careen through it all, dodging the brain-poppingly tense pedestrians pouring into the roads, in a sure, steady line towards home. I breathed in the Thames air over London Bridge as I left the City behind me – brackish and smelling of the sea on an incoming tide; slightly swampy on the way out. By the time I got home, I would be planted right back inside myself.

Cycling the city has given me total independence, from traffic, from my friends, from my partner, from my problems, from gravity. It takes the modest/pathetic power in my body and scales it up – with simple mechanical engineering not involving any external power source or emissions – into a roadworthy level of speed and efficiency. People are often shocked and bemused, or downright horrified, when they spot me cycling in heeled shoes. It is obvious they have never tried it, because if they did they would see how high heels, as long as they are not the type to slip off, are an almost ideal cycling shoe. They give optimum stability in the stop position, and traction advantage on launch. They also prevent pedal-foot slippage by acting as a backstop. Try it and you will find them much more versatile than toe clips.

During my pregnancy, I had pelvic pain. Walking was not possible. Riding was fine, though. It felt therapeutic on a muscular and skeletal level, as long as I went gently. I cycled right up to my due date. Like many Londoners (but not enough), I don't drive, so without the bike I would have been completely stuck.

When my son was about 11 months old, I knew he was ready to go on a bike with me. I introduced him to the Weeride baby bike seat, which sits right up in front, so the baby is positioned in between your loving arms. You can talk wonder into their ear as you ride, without shifting from your optimum riding position. The hand rest is like handlebars, so my baby felt he was controlling the bike, and was duly thrilled. He quickly grew very confident.

The unusual configuration surprised and delighted passers-by, who pointed and smiled and waved, and he grinned and waved at everyone in return.

When he was 15 months old I took him to Swaziland in southern Africa to visit family, and I took his Weeride with us. Together with my sister, her partner and their little daughter, we bicycled the mountain wilderness of the Malolotja National Park, stopping and not stopping through and among the rhebok and zebras, blesbok, wildebeest and eland. We pedalled among the butterflies, moths and dragonflies, swallows, cranes and ibis. At one point we sat down a short way from the water's edge, only to see a pair of gigantic, fearsome crocs just a few metres from where we sat. This is when you realise just how immediate the environment is when you're cycling.

It was a refreshing change of scene, and risk factors, for a pair of London cyclists. I was horrified at how fearful and de-skilled I was in an off-road environment.

As well as being a here-and-now city for me, the place where I continue to make discoveries and turn exciting new corners in my life, London also contains a parallel world of long, long ago memories. These are so prevalent that my mind doesn't bother to replay them any more. They are not bad memories. There are just so many of them.

Certain places just have thicker air for me. The past is like ghostly little hands pulling on me as I pass through. I'm thankful once again for my bike, which means I can glide through, free and light.

Like an ape swinging fast and sure from the treetops of a derelict memory,
I bike at speed through the streets from here to there,
There is a hidden world I am freewheeling on top of.
I cannot fully feel what is gone, and yet it is always shimmering
Beneath the surface of my experience:
I am the only seed who hasn't strayed,
But in my mind I have strayed so far from the past
That I can't remember who I was.
I just freewheel.

ED GRAY

SHIFTING SHAPES ON THE MILE END ROAD

Mile End Underground Station. This is where I arrive each morning to come to work in my studio, and where I leave to head back to Rotherhithe each evening. A microcosm of arrivals and departures, much like the East End itself.

I had made work about Mile End Park and Whitechapel before, but I'd never painted the scenes that greet me as I come up for air from the platform below. I stand in the station entrance and start to make sketches over a few days, as I usually do in any given location. I quickly realise that this time I want to work differently. I decide just to look at and memorise a different part of the scene, and then carry it with me to the studio to work on further. This way I hope the story will reveal itself to me over time.

I first notice the way Gary the newspaper seller is the anchor of the scene in the morning – chatting each day with anyone or simply watching people make their entrances and exits. In the evening the African preacher arrives. He cries out to the multitude that they "will be cast into the fires of hell for all eternity!" He spits out words to the tearful drunk in the old military greatcoat and the commuters of all faiths and none. Undeterred, he seeks only to cleanse them. Some 150 years ago William Booth's Salvation Army found a voice here preaching against the Demon Drink.

The East End has been a centre of faith ever since the 14th-century White Chapel gave its name to the area, so fire and brimstone have been burning the ears of East Enders for a long time. Even today the bells of the Whitechapel bell foundry and the PA system for the call to prayer from the East London Mosque are to be found within earshot of each other. New faiths have always come here with every new wave of arrivals across the seas – the Huguenots, the Jews, the Bengalis, the Irish. Each one lit with their own light in the darkness of a foreign land they would come to call home. Be it through persecution,

ARTIST CHRONICLING **LONDON**

economic necessity, desperation, dreams or simple curiosity, the Thames has brought many generations here. These migrants in turn have shaped the area to their own needs. As I climb to the top of the Tube station steps I look out at the long, straight Roman road that is now the Mile End Road.

Written on the whiteboard in the corner of the Tube station is the quote of the day, from Dolly Parton: "If you don't like the road you're travelling on, start paving a new one." An estate agent pauses to read the quotation – perhaps the message strikes a chord as he surveys the "luxury" new-builds for the latest influx of homebuyers and the changing skyline of the city. His cufflinks have "Buy" and "Sell" written on them.

A place of entrances and exits then as now, the Mile End Road of the 18th century would have been a very cosmopolitan place, proximity to the City making it a centre for shipping merchants, slave traders and insurance and financial men. People with experience of embarking on voyages that would take them to seek fortunes from every corner of the globe. One of the main maritime industries in Mile End was rope-making.

My eye is caught by the crest of the West Ham-shirted City worker on his way to a post-work match and a post-match pint. Two beating hammers symbolise the earliest incarnation of the team – workers who built ships to circumnavigate the colonised world.

New people bring new ideas and new ways of being. Dissenters have long found audiences in the East End. Sitting on a bin across from the preacher, an artist wistfully ogles a waiting girl as he holds a ready-made placard for a show nearby, at Robin Klassnik's "Matt's Gallery". The gallery has been exhibiting artists' work in the area since 1979. These days art is less about dissent and more a kind of secular religion. Many visitors to the East End book weekend tours to see backstreet urban frescoes.

The Stansted bus pulls up and an amorous couple are reunited, much to the annoyance of the harassed driver. New arrivals.

An artist climbs the steps to work, masking tape and a copy of *ArtReview* in his canvas bag.

An argument breaks out over spilt chips. The chips are down. A young army cadet leaves the barracks, stopping to pick up chicken from Perfect Fried Chicken.

Boudou yawns in his confectionery stall as a man helps a young pregnant mother carry a pram down the steps.

The metalwork on the steps begins to look like notes on a piano keyboard.

I watch the people entering and exiting the Tube station over a couple of months as I work on the painting. Each day I carry these shifting shapes back to the studio and through a fog of charcoal the characters take their places on the stage before me. I lay down layers of paint and somehow I begin to hear the rhythms of the city that I love.

Dame Zaha Hadid

Architect; twice-winner of the RIBA Stirling Prize and first female winner of the Pritzker Architecture Prize

LONDON'S UNIQUE POTENTIAL

I can say from my personal experience it is a very liberating experience living in London. My own work developed entirely because I live in this city. It is a very British situation; the UK has traditionally given a platform to those from around the world who want to research and innovate. London, in particular, has always welcomed and encouraged a tremendous degree of experimentation. What is very important to me as an architect is the remarkable knowledge and skills of the city's engineers and consultants. There is a uniqueness to London – anything you want, you can find someone in London with tremendous experience to advise you.

A seminal London figure for me was Peter Rice, an engineer with the design consultancy Arup. He was the first of his generation to match innovative engineering with new, untried ideas and concepts. We did a project more than 20 years ago at the Architectural Association where we drew lines through a map of the city and then travelled along these lines, documenting everything. It was a very interesting project because, first of all, it showed that certain components were aligned with each other, but that others – when you jumped from one level to next

– were tremendously varied. These extreme adjacencies are what make London so unique. It's a great city that has become very layered with traditions, histories and cultures.

I really like the brutalist 1960s and '70s buildings on the South Bank – the Hayward Gallery, the National Theatre, all that area. They're among the few examples of that style of work remaining in London. This architecture has fallen out of favour and most of it is being demolished, but it's actually some of the best architecture we have in London.

Unlike most European cities, London still has large gaps that allow for major urban intervention on an interesting scale. Look at the site for the 2012 Olympics, for example. We did a drawing more than 15 years ago about how London should be developed towards the east and it's fascinating to see this becoming a reality with the Olympics as a catalyst. It has offered the possibility of some very positive interventions with interesting solutions. There is tremendous potential here in London, and often the more radical it is, the more appropriate it is for the city.

Dame Zaha Hadid, 1950–2016

LAL HARDY

Founder of the New Wave tattoo studio, Muswell Hill

—

LONDON IN MY HEART

—

London, a city of so many constants yet so many changes. A place I love and sometimes hate!

My home for 57 years – a wealth of memories, the pubs, clubs, haunts and venues of my youth. The Lyceum packed with teddy boys and girls rockin' and rollin' the night away; the King's Road, Chelsea, with its punks and the Nutty Sound of Madness in Camden Town; rock nights at the Astoria and drinking nights at the Intrepid Fox, Soho.

The tiny little tattoo shop owned by Big Jock in King's Cross with its eclectic mix of clients, ladies of the night, rough tough hard-drinking men, tourists, thieves, criminals, lost souls, the lonely, runaways – a world of its own the likes of which most will never experience – a true education. So many pubs of London with their particular uniqueness and rich array of characters are being lost for ever.

The costers of Petticoat Lane, Tubby Isaac's shellfish stall, pie 'n' mash, Cockney rhyming slang, wheeling and dealing – that was Sunday mornings in Middlesex Street, along with the sad sight of the animals of the Club Row live animal market in my youth.

Nowadays I love early-morning London, before all the hustle and bustle starts – walking to work through some of the little hidden green spaces known just to locals, the flash of green as a woodpecker starts and makes his undulating flight, the urban fox strolling without a care.

I love the view on a clear day from Ally Pally looking across London's vast expanse. On a dark crisp night the view is equally stunning with the city illuminated against its dark backdrop.

I love the journey to White Hart Lane to see the Spurs, the anticipation on a derby day, the banter, the tension, the noise.

I love my red heart tattoo with London emblazoned across its banner.

I love that wherever you are from, if you make London your home you become part of it – WE ARE LONDON.

Sir John Hegarty

**Advertising executive; founder of Bartle Bogle Hegarty
and start-up brand incubator The Garage, Soho**

—

THE CREATIVITY OF SOHO

—

London started life as a trading city, sitting on the banks of the Thames. This has defined its character ever since. Open, inclusive and vibrant.

The face of London is the face of the world. Never locked in a moment of time but ever changing and evolving. And at the heart of this capital city is its creative character. Its freedoms and openness are a magnet to the persecuted and censored throughout the world.

Writers, artists, poets and thinkers have flocked to London, its great art schools and places of learning a source of inspiration.

But nowhere is this felt more than in the iconic square mile of Soho. The very name conjures daring, tolerance, irreverence and creativity.

In fact Soho is the most creative square mile in the world. To this day it has more creative people working in more creative professions than anywhere else. It's not surprising that so many other cities have tried to copy its name and nature. It embodies everything that is great about modern Britain and London. Rich with history, but also facing the future.

And of course it's located right in the heart of this city. Not sitting on some fringe, some forgotten suburb, but right in the centre. Reminding us all that this is what makes it special.

FERGUS HENDERSON

DEAN STREET

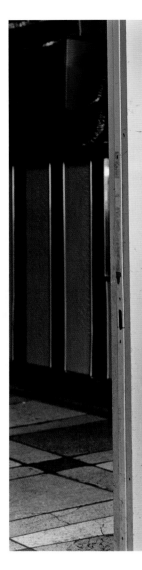

There are 100 metres of Soho, Dean Street to be precise, where there is much fun to be had. Maybe too much fun. Let's start at the Oxford Street end and work our way towards Shaftesbury Avenue: where better to commence than Quo Vadis? Here they make a fine gin martini; indeed they are so good it is hard to remember that you should never have more than two… Now let's continue down the road (but maybe today we'll miss the Groucho).

How has London changed, visitors often ask. Well, we could mention the shameful towers full of empty luxury flats, the traffic coming to a standstill due to the endless tinkering and digging up of the roads, and to top it all Soho is not what it used to be due to the rocketing rents. But all is not lost: I'm going to concentrate on some juicy morsels that remain changeless pleasures.

Let's begin with breakfast at Bar Italia over on Frith Street, a fantastic spot for watching folk start the day while you drink your coffee and chomp on a toasted panini. There is something very special about that moment when you have not quite committed to the day, and here is the perfect place to spend it.

As the hours advance you could do much worse than wander round to the French House pub, back on Dean Street. A bit like a zoo, they've got all the prime examples of Soho life drinking here. I used to have a restaurant above the pub and many of the old clientele have passed away, so it's rather like a place of preservation for endangered species. A charming pub, it is quite lively sometimes. But who is not up for a bit of lively every so often?

The day is moving on and so should you. Jump into a black cab, leaving Soho now as you head towards the City's Queen Victoria Street, to Sweetings, an old fish restaurant that could only possibly exist here in Britain. Start lunch with a tankard of Black Velvet, the perfect way to get your juices going. It was here that I proposed to my wife. What more can I say?

After lunch a stroll is required, so I recommend going to the middle of Waterloo Bridge for a fantastic view of London. The green roof of the Festival Hall, opposite which sits the Savoy…and now you've got this far, you really should pop into the American Bar for a hanky-panky. Most uplifting!

CHEF AND PROPRIETOR OF ST JOHN OF SMITHFIELD AND BREAD AND WINE, SPITALFIELDS

Anya Hindmarch

Handbag designer

—

GREEN CABMEN'S SHELTERS

—

I have a particular obsession with the green taxi huts of London, called Cabmen's Shelters; I call them taxi-man shelters. I first became aware of these shelters when I worked in an office opposite one and I wondered who was using them. The one opposite me would allow the hard hats – builders – to buy sandwiches; it helped to boost the trade of the people working there. They were quite anti the hard hats, though, because the shelters were built for the cabbies.

I got to know the lady who ran the taxi shelters, Tracy. She has very kindly allowed me to go and have breakfast in one of them. Sometimes I take a group of women I admire and think are interesting, and we have these breakfasts. It's a unique place to gather. Last time we had a woman who was running a prison rehabilitation scheme and *Vogue*'s Suzy Menkes. We have a real range of people from different industries. We were even involved in a short film about the shelters by Corinne van der Borch.

Tracy's father, husband and father-in-law were all hackney-cab drivers. She's told me about the cockney rhyming-slang names the shelters have, according to where they are located. The drivers who use the shelters have nicknames, too: the judge, the politician, the Pope…

There is U-shaped seating with a table that runs round the inside of the shelter: you can fit about ten people in there. They were designed in 1875 because, back when horses were pulling hansom cabs and then hackney carriages, the cab drivers were legally obliged to stay at the taxi stand while they were parked waiting. This often meant standing in freezing cold weather, and someone's horseman froze to death waiting outside. It was the Earl of Shaftesbury who set up a charity to construct the shelters. They're exactly the width of a horse and cart, no wider. There were 61 of them built, and the 13 that remain are all Grade II listed (indicating that they are of historic and architectural interest).

The idea of the shelters just fascinates me, and I actually produced a limited-edition diary that was inspired by these little buildings. We launched it in one of them.

It's one of my favourite things to do in London – go to a Cabmen's Shelter and have a great tea and breakfast. I love the architecture of the buildings themselves, but I suppose it's really about what black-cab drivers mean to London: they're very opinionated; they're the barometer of what London is thinking, in a way.

Leon Ho

Account Director, cyclist and joint-founder of Right Leg Rolled

---

RIGHT LEG ROLLED

Some people just want to get from A to B. I much prefer going via C, K and E. That is the magnetism of riding London…a paradoxical revelation that renders the magnitude of this city insignificant, yet opens up boundless probability, serendipity and adventure.

My journey into cycling is somewhat hackneyed. Privileged to have lived in East London as it tipped over from warehouse parties to garden parties, before the beautifully roguish T-bar became corrupted by the immaculately groomed hipster handlebar. Having faced off too many sunrises, like my surroundings, age and progression were catching up, or rather overtaking, gearless, brakeless. At a critical juncture in life's wayward journey, cycling was more than transportation, it was an antidote.

Riding unlocks adventure. Adventure is not just the great outdoors, those remote, dramatic landscapes, but it can be found hidden in the cracks and back streets of everyday London life. It is fuelling up with a four-ounce of freshly ground Ethiopian in Fitzrovia, unearthing wild swimming spots in Hackney Marshes, stumbling across the urban scything championships in

Walthamstow, rambling down the disused railway line of Parkland Walk, re-upping with a picnic by the bandstands of Hampstead Heath, gliding down the river on the cycle superhighway and rewarding yourself with a Crate IPA by Regent's Canal, amid a throng of wreckheads and runners.

That is because cycling is much more than speed, kilojoules and clocking up virtual goals. Whether fixed in perpetual motion to every bit of the tarmac or cruising carefree in top gear, it is reconnecting with the immediacy of the moment.

It is a mirror to our society, as rich and diverse, and evolving, as our capital. It is a subculture of courier crews, hippie tourers and geeky aficionados, grown to spawn hordes of commuters, middle-aged men in Lycra, and national treasures. It is vintage revivalists, hipster posturing and distance chasers. It is that knowing smugness with your unknown fellow riders. It is solace in the solitude and stimulation in the social. More than anything, it is momentary freedom from the swamping numbness of the city.

And at the same time it is just a steel frame, two wheels and a sturdy saddle.

Henry Holland

Fashion designer

LONDON'S OPEN SPACES

I grew up in the North of England, where more people tend to have their own garden and outdoor space. The lack of that personal space in London really pushes people to go out and experience public spaces in the city. There's nothing more depressing than going to my hometown and seeing the tired old playgrounds, neglected and gone to rust because people don't bother to use them.

In Lancashire, people walk their dogs on the moors, and there is far more beautiful scenery and open space in that respect, but there just aren't the same dedicated public spaces that there are with London parks. In complete contrast, I work next to London Fields, and the children's playground is never anything other than absolutely packed.

I've lived in London for 15 years. I used to live next to Primrose Hill but now I am near Victoria Park, and I think it's one of the most beautiful spaces. Public spaces and parks have been pivotal in forming my London experience: I spend a lot of time in them and I think the way people use them is one of the great things about the city.

Victoria Park is my favourite, for sure. I have a dog, so I need to be in the park every day, even in winter. You can go to the park, get a coffee and walk round – there's so much to see and do. I love the history surrounding the park, too: in the mid-19th century the East End was becoming overcrowded and the public petitioned Queen Victoria to create a royal park here. So it's a much-loved thing that she did for the people of East London and it bought her a lot of favour with them.

There's a Chinese garden there, which was a very trendy thing to have in the 1800s. There's so much history, but it's also just a really great place to hang out: you see people enjoying the outside in so many different ways – walking dogs, cycling, walking along the canal that runs right by it; people living in houseboats just next to the park. It has tennis courts, remote-control boat ponds, a paddling pool, memorial gardens…

The only thing it doesn't have is a lido, but it has a duck pond and amazing cafés. It's like a town in itself: it's such a lovely place to be.

DJ Hooch

DJ and founder of the UK B-Boy Championships

LONDON'S UNDERGROUND CLUB CULTURE

I lived in London all my life until recently and still consider myself a Londoner. I can go anywhere in London with my eyes closed: if I were blindfolded in a car, I'd know where I was going just by the direction.

I've achieved one of the longest running funk clubs, Funkin' Pussy, and the top level B-Boy event, the B-Boy Championships (the second longest running in the world, I think), which have both been a big part of my London life. But personally, I find what's special about London is the underground club culture. I used that word advisedly – it's become club culture, though it didn't start out that way.

I grew up in Kensal through the 1960s, '70s and '80s, so I grew up on sound stations and went to Carnival. Clubs were considered naff at the time, no one went to them – we went to warehouse parties and they were run by sound systems. In that culture, Norman Jay was a hero, definitely. Those boys – Norman Jay, Jazzy B, Soul II Soul – created those environments. The warehouse music scene was a world of underground parties.

Northwest London was a hotbed thanks to Carnival, so we had a lot of sound systems in the area, but it was a cross-London thing. Jazzy and those guys were from Camden, and we moved out of the west and started partying in East London – I can't tell you the amount of restaurants and bouji nightclubs today that were nothing but warehouses back then.

Sound systems and pirate radio created the best British music. That, to me, was the special part of London. We didn't go and watch bands; we followed sound systems. Apart from when you saw them at Carnival, they would be going round London. You'd find out about the sound systems through word of mouth or on pirate radio. I remember the Amityville House on the Hill party – they announced it on pirate radio, but nobody knew where it was. Just before it was supposed to start, they gave the address out – it was in Hampstead and everyone descended on this empty manor house. It had no proper stairways. A mass of people turned up.

There was another one like that, the White House in Kingston, with 2,000 people raving to soul, funk and reggae. It was amazing, that melting pot. This is before acid house. That kind of sensibility all came from that. It's where Talkin' Loud came from.

Mainstream radios have taken over a lot of the pirate studios. I used to listen to Tim Westwood and Trevor Nelson on Kiss FM before it was legal. There were a bunch of pirate radios based out in Harlesden – those were the ones you had to listen to if you wanted to know what parties were going on. Some of our guys were actually on them as well. It was a question of keeping it locked; all the best music was on there. Anything official, like the mainstream stations, nobody bothered with. That was all a bunch of bullshit.

That underground culture was amazing though. We were going to see Soul II Soul when they were doing gigs at places like the Cut. It'd be pitch black except for one light. The next

thing you know they're number one in America. But at the time it was strictly a London scene.

It was the most incredible time. Then, of course, acid house happened – it had all those sensibilities, it came from everything that had already gone on but with new music. There'd be one room of acid house and one room of rare groove, which was very '70s. S'Express were using old-school samples from disco records. So there was a fusion before it went strictly electronic and full-on dance. That whole time from the beginning of the '80s through to the early '90s, when it all got a bit over-exposed, was great, then it went back underground and I set up Funkin' Pussy.

That was my London. It's different now – those were my elders and from that I was inspired to start my club and the B-Boy Championships. I've been lucky enough to be involved in hip hop, rare groove, acid house, breaking… I'm still actively involved in club land and run my monthly nights. It's a proper underground club.

There is an underground scene now, but it's more controlled and owned. Grime is blowing up, but if it's all signed to major labels, it will all be controlled within a couple of years in a way that Drum 'n' Bass never was because it stayed away from the mainstream. Underground scenes are essential, but it takes balls to say, "No, we'll do it on our own."

Lucy Hopkins

Clown and performer

—

FANCY PIGEONS

—

Any visitor to London will quickly become aware of how many pigeons are hanging about in our public spaces. They may wonder how these surprisingly smart birds manage to survive in the city.

We once rooting racers fallen out of our race now. Companioning over millennia. Since Londonium and before then. Remember?

coo cooo ooo
tap tap
pitpitpit

I found you. Found you like before when we shared the rocks, your folk and mine sharing a living. Give and take, pitpitpit.

So many tides since then. Tide, moon, tree, comings and goings, around and around in the endless circle and you made your own cliff rocks, so many, smooth and shiny reaching up into the top wind. Less nest crag but ok, ok, everything ok, friend (why the spike and net, friend, why? but ok). We're bridgeunder and roof cavity, like the dovecote, friend, remember the dovecote? A cote on every home once! We're searching for them, friend, giz a crumb. Giz a bit o' pizza. When you're finished, friend, no rush. No fear, friend, for history bond is unbreakable like sandwich crispybacon and must be swallowed whole.

Crabbit's searching, but he never gets a bite. Dalion's after Nora, she's greased but perfect fantail the colour of an overcasting, he's got the throat on again, all throat and no action Dalion, all iridescent violet-green neck and shimmering Dragon.

Duck and bob, give it the circle, cooo coo. Scratchtoe curled under and a line of us bunching over Edith Cavell. Fortitude Humanity Sacrifice Devotion. It's a community of sorts, it's a roost, isn't it?

Jag's got a biscuit. Lift and flip-twitch it overhead.

pitpitpit
tagga tagga tagga pit
tantantan across the flagstone
brooo brooo brootal

Jag's got the cobfoot. Tangle in a line got him, once it's round there's no unwinding. Now the long way to hobblehood for him. Soon he'll be a hobbledog like Dawkin. Dawkin's got both grippers proper robbed, landed himself a glue patch and bam, both stumpers in one.

cobcobcob

Keep calm, cob on and soar on the ragwing over city cliff, flatterflatter shap shap shap, doves on the doorway, shadowdove, rockbird, dragonbird, shadowdragon.

Shrunken dragons now, friend.

Greasy head scragneck cobfoot cheesegrease spewpat. Might be something here in this tiny crack of pave. We could all be a bit healthier, couldn't we, friend?

pickpickpick

Racing roosting homing home
Tagga tagga tagga over the rocks to landing
tracing the ever-same path in our sky, settle on
the flat grey cliffs
For a moment
Settle pick
Settle pitpitpit
Settle pick pick gangangan flatterflatt up up up

again
Shadowdove rockbird racing home coming
home, here it is home, here we are together,
together, pickpick. Is this home? Is this together?

Look me in the amber dazzler and remember me,
friend.

pickpick
pitpitpit

Poppy Jackson

Actionist artist

GREENWICH FOOT TUNNEL

Attracted by its interesting history and unusual location below the river, I first visited Greenwich Foot Tunnel in 2010 for my performance-art project *Liminal Bodies*. The tunnel then became one of my favourite liminal spaces; somewhere that exists as a transitory "between" space, crossing a boundary and joining two distinct places but belonging to neither. The river water seeping into it gave the place animated and lifelike qualities, the fluorescent lighting reflected on the shiny glazed tiles creating a surreal, dreamlike atmosphere. Transiting through the tunnel's historic circular architecture as an underwater pedestrian symbolised to me all the stages of a rite of passage, which is how I view my own performances. It manifested physically the intense feeling of being within my performances – uncertain yet secure within the flux, buzzing with inspiration along a journey of transformation from one state or place to another.

Two glazed domes above ground form the threshold to the Foot Tunnel. These entrances house huge wood-panelled, 90-capacity lifts, which were previously operated by attendants with transistor radios that crackled during the descent underground. As soon as the lift doors open into the long tubular passageway, the stark change in humidity and temperature hits the skin and fills the lungs. You can smell the river through the tile-lined walls as the Thames above drips through in places, creating painterly stains on the walls and small stalactites that hang from the ceiling.

The tunnel is classed as a public highway, so it's kept open 24 hours a day. It follows an ancient ferry crossing that connects the classical architecture of Greenwich to the residential and then financial districts of the Isle of Dogs. The 370 metres of passageway dips down under the Thames at the *Cutty Sark*. I've heard people commenting on their way through that it is creepy and grotty, but I enjoy the unnerving sensation and the way it instantly transports you into an uncanny psychological state, heightening awareness of all the senses. It was built in 1902 in a U-shape, and the acoustics inside create a long echo effect – what sounds like a stampeding football team turns out to be one small boy bouncing a yellow ball off the sides.

A Second World War bomb damaged the northern end, causing the diameter to be reduced substantially in this section by thick steel inner repairs which leak. The ground is wet here, and there are wires and cables running overhead to electronic signs displaying messages about behaviour, sent from computers monitoring passenger activity. Other signs tell you that the tunnel is not a road and not to spit. All interesting material to an artist who works with her body in the public realm.

Ascending from this sensory experience, at ground level you find yourself in a leafy riverside park, where in summer families from many nationalities enjoy picnics. The exit opens out to a friendly kiosk, that I was pleased to find sells my favourite dark chocolate teacakes at 50p each.

NORMAN JAY

CARNIVAL

I've loved London with a passion: everything about it; warts and all. Having been fortunate enough to visit most of the major cities around the world, I'll take London any day. It offers so much in terms of history and culture. To a young teenager in the 1970s and into the '80s, no city offered the range of nightlife quite like London.

You used to get a ticket that allowed you to jump on and off the London buses all day – it was called the Red Rover. I used that in my formative years to get to know London. It's one of the reasons London Transport discontinued it – it was too popular. In the late '60s, early '70s, when I went as a kid, it was a fantastic way to spend the day. It was 15 or 16 pence, I think.

The one consistent love for me when it comes to London, however, is Carnival: going as a teenager and then eventually being part of the Carnival for over 30 years.

The first time I went I would have been about nine or ten, and I was with my Mum and Dad and aunt and uncle. I remember not really understanding what it was all about, and not really wanting to be there. I was born in Notting Hill and didn't know anything about the old country. Carnival was a fantastic spectacle, but I didn't culturally connect with it. It was a much smaller event then.

As a teenager, though, I got driven back into it when I went on my own or with friends. It was an amazing thing to be happening on the streets of London at that time. It was a very heavy, political era in the late '70s: the National Front was on the rise, the police were more than heavy-handed... Just putting it into context, it was a different culture pervading then. Things are so much better now.

Looking back on it now, London was still suffering post-World War II trauma. I can remember playing on the bombsites

DJ AND **CARNIVAL VETERAN**

in and around Notting Hill. It was a grandiose place that had fallen on hard times between and after the war, and now it's reverting back to type. It was always affluent, with the poor working-class living on the outskirts. They were just finishing the construction of the flyover at that time. They cleared huge swathes of Notting Hill. It was bleak, with not a lot of work around.

I first played the Carnival in 1980 – four years after the major riots of '76, which I was part of. I didn't go for the following year, it felt too risky, but then I plucked up the courage – well, not so much the courage… There was nothing else on offer; there was nothing else free. Going to the Carnival, seeing what was happening, lifted something in me. I thought, "I'd love to be part of this", but not playing the traditional music that Carnival was known for. I liked reggae and calypso, but I really liked soul and disco, which was the biggest music at the time, and I liked feel-good dance music. And Carnival for me didn't offer that. So I just thought: there's a window of opportunity here, maybe that is something I can offer them.

Britain was still quite tribal then: a lot of my mates were first-generation punks – like my wife. I loved the UK for its style tribes. You had the punks, the new romantics, all my old mod mates, my scooter-boy mates… I loved all of that. Having been part of all these different social groups, I felt I was on a mission to attract them to Notting Hill Carnival. The perception of Carnival was very negative with the media then. And from my perspective it was very backward-looking, parochial; almost an anachronism. But it was "ours", so it was down to us to change that perception and I consciously set out on the road to do that.

I'm semi-retired from Carnival now. The steamroller of redevelopment has changed things, and there's no way we could go back to the spot we used to play. It's now "affordable housing" for the rich. Land in London is at a premium… It's where there's money to be made.

I've had a good innings, though – 33 years I've played Carnival. It's been a long road, and an enjoyable one: Carnival has become an incredible institution, and will always hold some of my fondest memories of London.

Dom Joly

Comedian and film-maker

THE COW

It shouldn't have worked. A pseudo-Irish bar run by Albanians just on the right side of the Westbourne railway tracks. It shouldn't have worked…but it did. For ten years or so the Cow, on Westbourne Park Road, was my local, my office, the place where I assembled hangovers and then tried to get over them.

I'd drink Magners on ice (before it was trendy) or just pints and pints of Guinness. The food was sensational. From one tiny hob and a crusty oven would come restorative plates of bangers and mash or succulent loins of lamb – assuming you didn't stick to endless rounds of Whitstable oysters.

Best of all was the people-watching. Grab a rare table outside and watch *le tout* West London cruise past. Inside, the clientele was a smoky hotchpotch of ageing locals, members of the boho-chic establishment and a decent standard of celebrity. Nick Cave could often be seen in the far corner. Sinéad O'Connor would waft through. I once got so drunk with Damien Hirst that I forgot to ask him to doodle and sign my napkin.

Trigger Happy TV was basically born there. Long drunken nights were spent staring at the painting that took up a whole wall. It was a surreal pastoral scene depicting creatures of the sea as landlubbers. Prawns fox-hunting, fish hosting dinner parties…that landscape warped my mind in a seriously good way. I still wander through it in my dreams.

I haven't been back for years. Last time I went, Japanese tourists had started to visit. They'd perch awkwardly on the high stools, endlessly photographing their food as their baby-doll legs dangled pointlessly in the void.

Our little corner of Notting Hill was changing. The bankers were moving in. All the pubs went gastro, while shops became boutiques. The Cow looked at these changes with a wry smile. The atmosphere, the clientele, the vibe were part of an old Notting Hill that has almost disappeared – swallowed up by wheatgrass-munchers and Starbucks clusters. All things must pass.

Dylan Jones

Editor in chief, *GQ* magazine

LONDON RULES

London is the most dynamic city in the world today. Sure, it has always been an international hub, always been at the centre of things, but it has never sizzled like it sizzles today. Sure, we are in the middle of a Brexit cycle, but then so is everyone else. In the 21st century London has become the most powerful, the most go-getting, the most culturally focused city on earth. Nowhere else comes close. Not New York. Not Paris. Not Shanghai. Not Hong Kong.

It is all about London. Still.

Forget about Brexit.

Other cities in the UK make grand claims and have their devotees and their champions, but Manchester, Edinburgh, Leeds and the rest pale before the might, sight, sounds, churn and fire of London. And those who disagree are just expressing the politics of envy. Our grand city is the heart, soul, muscle and brain of Britain, the principal reason for its greatness.

And it's never been as great as it is today.

London is the one true global cultural megalopolis, the one cocksure city-state, and we need to shout about it from the top of every tall building in town. The closer the social historian, cultural bellwether or hack gets to their own times, the more difficult it is for them to be sure that they have grasped what is essential about their period. This is largely a matter of vantage point, as some features of the pattern may not yet even be visible. But trust me, having lived in the city for 40 years, I know what I say to be true. Indisputably so.

Nowadays London might not be the biggest city in the world (Tokyo/Yokohama can claim that crown), yet this powerful and distinctive place is as full of architectural riches as it's ever been. The décor and architecture of important London buildings once seemed to represent a conscious desire to be part of an imaginary immemorial city, whereas these days every new building wants to look like the future, encouraging a nostalgia for an age yet to come. As London gets bigger, so it seems to be raising the bar. As Anthony Sampson said in *Anatomy of Britain*, back in pre-swinging 1962, "Bigness has strengthened the lure of London."

Many people suffer a transmogrification when they reach the metropolis, reinventing themselves in a way that simply isn't possible in the provinces. Of course, anyone can reinvent themselves when they arrive in a big city – just look at how Bob Dylan and Joe Strummer, two of the most powerful icons in the rock canon, *jhuzzed* up and downgraded their backgrounds when they hit town – but London seems to actively encourage it. New York applauds anyone who arrives and makes a success of themselves, whereas London inspires people to amplify their personalities. Those already here will take great delight in knocking the newcomers down a peg or two, but that doesn't mean that amplification isn't encouraged.

London life nowadays is a lifestyle, a kaleidoscopic, polyphonic theme park across 32 boroughs (33 if you count the separately

governed City of London) and nine travel zones. It houses grand hotels, dive cocktail bars, world-renowned design galleries, bohemian indie clubs, family-owned bistros, esoteric independent retailers, theatres, gentrified trophy parks, state-funded public art and reclaimed open spaces, a cavalcade of consumerism and participatory art.

London is a more exciting city now than it's ever been. Comparison may be the thief of joy, and it might be invidious to square London off against New York, Milan or Paris – which is heavier, a ton of feathers or a ton of gold? – but right now there is no other city in the world like

it. Which makes me think that maybe we should turn London into a city-state, or a citadel. Not to keep people out, and not to keep them in, but to celebrate the fact that London deserves to be recognised as the most important city on earth. Historically, places such as Rome, Athens and Carthage were honoured with this status, but these days the term only really applies to Singapore, Monaco and Vatican City, and possibly Hong Kong and Dubai.

But isn't our treasured city better than all of them put together?

I'd say so. In fact, I think I just did.

Princess Julia

DJ, music writer and model of clubland renown

FRICTION AND SPARKS

Falling over, getting back up again, we do that a lot in London and have a right good laugh about it. It's all a bit seamy; on the other hand everything's the height of glamour. Walk into a pub, down a street, pass somebody famous; look sideways and glimpse someone done up to the nines or a stinky beggar on the cadge for anything. Look up and see a grey London sky full of doom and at the same time a strange optimism envelops you, changing skylines and beautiful brutal reality.

No money…? Poverty breeds creativity, that's what they say. Nevertheless perhaps it's true, especially in London where people seem to gravitate toward seeking out an identity more vital than the one they've left behind. I did the same, left North London and headed uptown, central, on the Piccadilly Line. London's built on a by-line: I heard someone say that somewhere – I think it's true because there's a certain energy here in London.

Bobby Kasanga

Founder of Hackney Wick Football Club, whose members are encouraged to offer their services to the community

HACKNEY MARSHES

There is a place on the east side of London which is like a Mecca, a church, a synagogue or a temple to many. The only thing it can be described as is a plain grass field with no major beautiful landscape.

How can a plain green field, sat in between a motorway and a council estate, mean so much to thousands of people across generations?

It's because when you add the white markings, the corner flags, the countless goalposts, the goal nets and then the thousands of adults and children kicking their beloved "pig's bladder" up and down, it becomes not just a plain field – it's the utopia of grass-roots football.

Of all perfumes, aftershaves and exotic fragrances that adorn our TV screens over the Christmas period, I ask if, among them, there is a greater scent than that of muddy boots, sweat and the great outdoors.

This may sound extreme, but the Hackney Marshes are to the local community what insects are to humans.

Are you asking what the hell is he talking about? Has he gone crazy? Humans? Insects?

Look deeper and you will see my point.

What I am trying to say is that the Hackney Marshes are at the beginning of the food chain, which results in billions of people across the globe tuning in to their TV screens on a weekly basis to watch their idols running up and down other more evolved (yet still grass) fields, kicking a pig's bladder.

The English, the Europeans, the Africans, the West Indians, the Asians, the North and South Americans and the Arabs all gather around every weekend, walking on their own, cycling in twos, five in a car, sixteen in a coach, with multicoloured kits, talking team tactics in multiple languages. There are bandages, tape, Deep Heat, shin pads, water bottles and faces of joy or thunder (depending on match results), but every week they will be back.

You can reach Stansted Airport by nipping down the nearby A12 to the M11 motorway, but why would you travel abroad when you can have a taste of the world every weekend at the Hackney Marshes? This place embodies multicultural London at its best.

It is no coincidence that this seemingly plain field is located in London. Just another reason why this is the greatest city in the world.

Bernie Katz

Manager of the Groucho Club

—

SOHO'S SECRET STREETS

—

Soho – a playground for the over-30s. Those in their 20s go there too, but my advice is to wait another decade. Soho is a tolerant, vibrant village, best visited at night.

I stand on the rooftop of the Groucho Club, where I have spent the last 22 years – this fine but frantic house stands firm on Dean Street, number 45. A gust of cold wind billows its way past, reminding me of the season that is yet to give us its finale.

I stand tall like Zeus looking down from Mount Olympus; shielded by a silk olive-green curtain, I can see the streets that are missed by visitors of the day. Even locals are not always aware of their existence, but exist they do – they are the secret streets of Soho.

Using my deity's eye from the highest peak I see Bourchier Street – a street that after twilight should be avoided if travelling alone. Some have not taken that advice and have never been seen again.

Ah, a nicer street I can spy while on tiptoe, taking care not to dance too close to the edge of this rooftop I know so well – the mews just behind Duck Lane, off Berwick Street. A place where I have had many merry Christmas parties, turned on the Christmas lights and left at dawn, adorned with sunglasses in winter to ease the morning's rude, violent interruption.

As I twist around to be sure that no secret street has been unveiled, I see a tiny gateway with a row of houses of plenty, shielded by a dominant black iron Victorian gate and hidden from the busy naked eye – this little beauty is just off Greek Street.

Across to the other side of my now mountain I see Brewer Street. Then past Peter Street but just before Glasshouse Street there's a twist where you can park your car and see the bright lights (if you like that sort of thing) of Leicester Square. Quickly turning on my heels, if I put my hand on my brow to cover the daytime light, I just about see Old Compton Street – home to an ever-changing row of shops, cafés and restaurants, not forgetting the Prince Edward Theatre – as we skip along the sunny side of the street past Shaftesbury Avenue. Hey presto, there's a winding number of lanes that meet each other and lead to a mini Jurassic Park for the children of Soho to play in, an overgrown mass of bushes that are now small ugly trees joined by grass just as tall. A tip to all parents – don't let your children play there.

Now back to Berwick Street Market and in the middle stands an old off-key tower block, once home to a famous Soho character, the journalist Jeffrey Bernard. Many new, full, half, eclipse moons ago he would take tea at the Groucho Club. Only satisfied when seeing double, he would summon me to wheel him home in his wheelchair and, as we merrily shouted at one another, we would come face to face with the tall white monster of a building that still stands today and that Jeffrey once called home. Well, behind this is a short cut, not so secret but very hidden. If you don't know it's there, then you don't know it's there. And as we come to the end of this adventure, have you noticed that there are no walkways called something or other "road"?

Take care and hope to see you on Dean Street – after the moon has replaced the sun, that is.

DSC_9536.JPG   DSC_9549.JPG   DSC_9569.JPG   DSC_9589.JPG   DSC_9593.JPG

Cecilia Knapp

Writer, performer and poet

—

THE 24-HOUR LAUNDERETTE IN MILE END

—

The 24-hour launderette in Mile End smells of
washing powder.
It can't smell of anything else.
It reminds me of resting my head on your chest,
It reminds me of being held.
 People have made their mark on the
wooden benches with felt tips
And permanent markers.
Fuck the fear, it says.
Fuck everything and run.
 You always used to tell me I was the
strongest one.
I work in a pub where the men refer to the
loves of their lives as "The Wife".
Where Thursday nights see City boys in artificial
lights
 Drinking lager like a right
And chasing skirt like it's their life's work.
 And Terry. Who took an early retirement.
Told me he was sick of fighting other people's battles.
 He always leaves his tips in coppers
And, as he sips,
Bravado ebbs away in shudders,
All come to nothing.
He told me once that he was lonely,
Among the midweek broken hearts,
All drowning in a wine glass.
 Then there's Jack.
In his flat cap,
Sturdy as my Dad's toolbox,
Wrinkles like a crackling radio,
With a smile stuck somewhere between night
and morning.
He tells me about the war. Like he hasn't told me

50 times before
And I'm not sure if he even fought, but that's not
the point.
He has half a pear cider and each time I tell him I
like his trainers,
He says thanks, they're from Watney Market,
And calls me mate with all the tenderness of a Sunday.
 And I remember you, in that moment, gently
smoking by the kitchen door,
The green behind the hazel of your eyes.
How your front teeth weren't a perfect line so you
had this crooked smile,
Like mine,
And all our arguments, confident from Sunday
night wine.
All our times.
 Jack tells me some days he can see the
sadness behind my eyes, but I just smile
And say, "Half a cider?"
And he says, "Yes, mate, you'll be fine."
 He asked if I believed that those you've lost
watch over you.
I told him I had to.
And though he told me he thought that God is dead,
I once saw him cross himself,
Emboss his name upon his chest,
Some inexplicable paradox, or just uncertainty
at best.
 "And what about love?" he said.
"What love?"
So I told him that my grandmother's wedding ring
Was so eroded by time
And got so thin
That it had to be replaced.

But that I don't even know if that type of love exists.
    I saw the kindness in his face and he said
I should give it a try.
    But right now, for me, love is knock and run
in a cul-de-sac
And sunburn on the soles of your feet,
Neat whisky with no water and admitting defeat.
    He told me pain means I'm not made of
stone. I said, I know.
He said I've got a long way to go
And that my heart is still beating under all the
mess,

His eyes like lovers in separate beds,
    Desperate heads in hands or the boy too
close to the edge,
Searching for a rest.
He squeezed my hand. Never give up, he said,
Turned on his heel and left,
Empty half-pint glass on the bar ledge.
And me,
Stood left with a half smile.
    Back here in the launderette,
The tumble dryer stops spinning but I don't
notice for a while.

Charles Landry

Authority on the use of imagination and creativity in urban change; author of *The Creative City* and *The Art of City Making*

LONDON RESONATES RICHLY...

London resonates richly. Its sensescape is immersive and diversity immense. Take the names of streets as an instance. London has more than any city I know and each conjures up a different sensation. Some sound ordinary and others extra-ordinary. Some quite grand and others rather twee or cute. Some sound formal and others informal. There are old-fashioned ones and unusual ones pointing to the future. With some you feel the straight lines and big vistas; with others the sensuous curves and intimate spots. You know there are deep layers, history and complexity to London.

Close your eyes and visualise these London landscapes, the shapes they evoke, their social make-up, their origins, their aspirations and the lives lived. Bob Marley Way in Lambeth and in contrast Browning Close in Little Venice. Charles II Street in Westminster or Back Lane NW3. An avenue mostly sweeps gracefully and Northumberland Avenue differs starkly from the short and stubby Niagara Avenue in Ealing, even though the real Niagara Falls are dramatic and wild. Every name represents a journey, a history, a story. Mandela recalls those magic moments of freedom, yet Mandela Way in Southwark is best known as the home of a Royal Mail delivery centre. History so often is lost, although names still echo through time. Drury Lane summons up vibrant theatre life, but in fact now looks dull. It is also where the first J Sainsbury opened in 1869 and the Workers' Educational Society was based in the 1840s. With many names you wonder why. Cheapside – was it cheap? Knightsbridge – did knights cross over a bridge? Percy Circus in Islington – did Percy have a circus?

There are crosses as in Charing Cross, rows as in New Row, courts and quads, not to forget the squares, closes, gates, alleys, lanes, walks, paths, hills and endless places called street or road where some are new and some are old. Think of Old Road, Lewisham, or New Road, Whitechapel.

This reminds you that for The Knowledge London's black-cab drivers need to know the over 60,000 streets within a 10-kilometre radius of central London. They provide a vast array of possibilities with nature everywhere in evidence. Yet how many acacias or walnut trees did London really have, considering the number of Acacia or Walnut Avenues? Or did local councils offer up these names so residents could dream of a more idyllic, non-existent past? Some have been more heartless. Alpha Grove E14 is now a bland Alpha Road and Alma Grove SE1 now Alma Road.

Yet London's changing global life is running ahead of its past, most visibly in the suburbs. Will Brent's Euro Close NW10 change its name after Brexit? How about another form of reincarnation, like in Karma Way in Harrow? Or fitting into the trend for spirituality – I think here of Yoga Way in Sutton. But Christianity still holds sway – there are several hundred London streets with "Church" in them. That monopoly is eroding, though, as seen in Masjid Lane in Tower Hamlets, which uses the Arabic term for mosque, or Khadija Walk in Lewisham to honour Mohammed's first wife, the first person after him to convert to Islam. Clapham by contrast must have had a philosophy graduate in its naming department, witness Aristotle Road SW4 and Plato Road SW2. Street names continue to surprise, reflecting their times, place and circumstances.

James Lavelle

Musician, DJ and producer; pioneer of the London rave scene

—

THE SCENE

—

For me, growing up in Oxford in the 1980s, it was all quite grey and boring. You had only four TV channels and very little information stimulation. That feeling was only emphasised by the fact that Oxford is placed between Bristol and London, and it was all happening in those two cities.

I started going to London aged 14 to do martial arts. Carnaby Street. That area of Soho was really important to me in terms of getting into music. Just going to Soho, you had right there what was going on with the music world: that was how I discovered record shops and clothes.

Hip hop was the defining sound for me as a teenager. Soho back then was just alive with independent dance-record stores: there would be music from America and music from the UK that was coming out of the clubs – a mixture of hip hop, early house, techno and soul. For me, just being around somewhere like Berwick Street and Carnaby Street – with record stores like Bluebird, Red Records, Groove Records – was incredible. It was a golden era of discovery for me going to these stores; it felt very alien. You'd go to these environments and it would be very hard core: it was a very mixed-race scene, very alive; the mental culture of the time just doesn't exist any more because DJ culture has changed. If you didn't get *the* record, you weren't going to be the DJ of the night. There was immense competition to get *the* record. It was very street and very working class. The energy was quite intense for someone who came from middle-class Oxford.

Those stores don't really exist so much any more: it was Camden and Portobello Road, mainly, that you went to then. At Camden there would be Soul II Soul and Zoom; there'd be independent record stores; they'd be selling clothes on the street. You could find amazing vintage record stores, clothes stores, vintage furniture stores, a lot of which has now disappeared onto the Internet. I ended up working at one of those shops – I worked at Bluebird on Edgware Road.

When I first came down to London I was still living in Oxford, where we didn't even have pirate radio stations: you had to go out and buy cassettes; you had to go to those places if you wanted to get sneakers or T-shirts or to find out where raves were; you just had to go there. That process created your cultural integration with people and it was how you met people along the way. That's how I ended up working with Mo' Wax. That's something that still exists but it's very different now.

Portobello retains a bit of the same feel – it still has Honest Jon's Records, where I went to work. But then there were all these amazing individual boutique places where you could find culture. If you walk down Camden High Street now, it's all sneakers shops and Arctic Monkey T-shirts. Back then there was a massive array of things going on. So many things have influenced that change – from the economy to shopping going online.

You could walk around, at that time, on a weekend and you'd see everybody: you'd see

all the different crews from the different areas in London. The scene was mainly West London, Soho and a bit of Brixton and Hoxton Square – where the clubs were. There was Dingwalls in Camden, the Wag in Soho… You'd see all the DJs: if you were on Portobello, you'd see people like Norman Jay; if you were in the West End you'd see people like Tim Westwood and the hip-hop crews and house DJs. That scene that I came into was, essentially, counter-culture; it wasn't something you saw on your mobile phone. It was just this amazing thing, to see these heroes of yours walking around buying records. I feel lucky to have experienced that.

Ciara Lawrence

Campaigns Support Officer, Mencap

LONDON SHOWS

My name is Ciara Lawrence and I have a learning disability. I have worked for Mencap for 16 years and I currently work in the Campaigns and Activism Team as a Campaigns Support Officer. My job is to help campaign for the rights of people with a learning disability and their families.

Mencap is the UK's leading learning disability charity. We aim to help people with a learning disability and their families to live a fulfilled life as much as possible, with the right support. We also run campaigns and fund-raise to make sure we can carry on Mencap's good work into the future.

When I was growing up I was bullied at my local mainstream school for a long time because I was different. I found it hard to learn new things. I was singled out and picked on; I was called horrid names and excluded from friendship groups in my class. I was laughed at. It made me feel so angry and worthless and I believed all the nasty things that people said to me. It had a huge emotional effect on me. Sometimes I just wanted to be ill so I didn't have to face it. To have a learning disability was hard enough without being bullied. I used to make myself ill every day so I didn't have to go to school.

During the time I was bullied, the only thing I felt I could turn to was pop music and musical theatre songs, because I always loved to sing as a kid. I would come home from school, turn on my stereo and play songs that made me feel safe and happy. It was an escape from what I was feeling.

I started singing in the school choir and we did summer production shows which I really enjoyed. I was introduced to musical theatre songs and I fell in love with Andrew Lloyd Webber musicals.

My first London West End theatre trip was to see *Joseph and the Amazing Technicolor Dreamcoat* at the London Palladium in London for my 11th birthday. My Mum took me to see it and I saw Philip Schofield star as Joseph!

Music has been very important to me in my life: it has helped me to get through some dark times growing up. During those times I turned to the music role models that I really liked, like Kylie Minogue because her songs were positive.

It was my love of music that brought me close to my cousin Dave Evans, who is best known as The Edge from the Irish rock band U2. When I was growing up, he and I used to see each other when I went on holidays to Ireland. He always made sure I was looked after and was included in his life. He became a Mencap Ambassador in 2009. He even took me to the Brit Awards that year and took me backstage to meet Kylie Minogue, as he knew I was such as big fan of hers. I chatted to her about being bullied at school and how her music had helped me. Meeting her was a dream come true!

When I was a teenager, I started going to pop concerts at London venues like Wembley Arena. One of my best memories is being a huge Boyzone fan when I was 13 and my family arranging for me to go and meet the Boyzone boys backstage before their concert. I had the night of my life and got to enjoy it just like anyone else. Over the years I have also been a VIP Guest at U2's London gigs at Wembley Stadium, Earl's Court and the O2 Arena, which are just amazing!

As a person with a learning disability, I feel safe and accepted in London because no one knows me and I can be myself while being out and about.

Don Letts

DJ and film-maker; founder member of Big Audio Dynamite

—

CULTURE CLASH

—

"London is the place for me"
– Sung by Calypso king Lord Kitchener, when he arrived in the UK on the *Empire Windrush* in 1948.
   "Fings Ain't What They Used to Be"
– Sung by Max Bygraves in London in 1960.
   Those two lyrics sum up my thoughts on what makes London great. It's the influx of different cultures that has made this city what it is. It's what makes London swing, and I think I'm a product of that. I jokingly tell tourists I'm what London looks like now.
   I proudly describe myself as first-generation black British. A large part of who I am today is being a Londoner. I grew up in Brixton and now live in Kensal Rise. Where I grew up was a sign of the multicultural way Britain was headed, typified by the Notting Hill Carnival, which I've been going to for about 45 years.
   I've got some incredible memories of living in London: I remember sitting on top of Parliament Hill and watching Ally Pally burn down with Joe Strummer; seeing Bob Marley at the Lyceum and befriending him soon after; and being on the front line of the Notting Hill riots in the late 1970s. I remember DJ-ing at the Roxy Club, the very first punk rock live venue in the UK. The punk bands would be playing their fast and furious live sets and in between that I'd be playing dub heavy reggae. Out of this came punky reggae party, typified by bands like the Clash, the Slits, and later on John Lydon's Public Image Limited. We were turning each other on through our respective cultures. I was in the middle of all of that.

My first stage performance, which happened accidentally, was with Patti Smith at the Hammersmith Odeon back in 1975. She was a big reggae fan and we became friends when she stayed in London during her stint at the Roundhouse. Patti heard I was mates with the reggae artist Tapper Zukie and asked if we'd like to come to see the show. So she was doing her thing up on stage and we were watching from the wings. All of a sudden she pulls Tapper on stage and puts a guitar in his hands. Now Tapper was an emcee and he can't play so I gave him a signal to play air guitar. So he's "playing" air guitar and I'm killing myself with laughter in the wings when Patti suddenly pulls me on stage and puts a microphone in my hand. This was a problem because, as everybody knows, there's no such thing as an air microphone! Luckily for me I had my dark glasses on, which hid the fact I was terrified. I started to "rap" in my heaviest Jamaican "slanguage" so the audience couldn't tell I didn't know what the hell I was going on about. Next thing I know, I look to my right and Tapper's "playing" air guitar, then I look to my feet and Patti's writhing on the floor. With a lot of hindsight, I can now see that that was probably the real birth of punky reggae party.
   Music and the cultural creativity that comes with it are the main reasons I love London, but there's a correlation between the current economic state of the city and its creative output. You look at art now and a lot of it's shit – because many of these young artists are now living with

their parents. I mean, how rebellious can you be if you're living with your mum?!

We are in danger of gentrification ruining the nation: London is fast becoming an economically walled city whereby if you ain't got enough money in your bank account, you ain't gonna get to go to the party. All the people who make this city work and help it to run are being priced out to the fringes. They spend all their wages going backwards and forwards to serve the well-heeled. This won't end well. You can only fuck with people for so long.

All that said, I still think London's the greatest city in the world and there are some exciting pockets of creativity – the multicultural clash brings it out through the music, the food, the fashion and the language. Ultimately, I think it's by embracing and understanding our differences that we'll become closer as people. The influx of different cultures has changed the very idea of what it means to be British and nowhere is this demonstrated better than in my hometown. There are rough bits in there, of course. I mean ain't nothing all beautiful: you've got to have some ugly in it. But London is a laboratory for multiculturalism and it wouldn't be so prominent on the world stage without it.

At the end of the day you can't have output without input and I get plenty of that in London because I'm tapping into the culture mix which, in turn, inspires me to create and informs my very being. I love this city with all its greys and I'm here to tell you: if you don't love the greys in London then you don't really love London at all.

Ben Lambert

Creative Director of the Listeners Project

—

Natasha Coleman

Executive Producer of the Listeners Project

—

BEHIND THE WALLS

—

Natasha: I think one of the things that we enjoy most about London is its hidden spaces, the mysterious nooks and crannies behind its closed doors. In some ways it's like having a relationship with the city. As time goes by, living side by side, slowly you start to see the hidden depths, the hidden corners of a person, and get to know them intimately. It's the same every time we are invited into an old building – suddenly London opens up a little more.

Ben: As film-makers for the Listeners Project we've been really lucky to open the doors on some curious locations in London. So far we've been invited inside the walls of a 1960s upholstery shop, the BBC Television Studios, an old glass factory that was the set for *Batman*, and most recently a mannequin factory – all of them due for renovation or demolition.

Natasha: It's very easy to walk past these buildings, charging to get to work, lost in your thoughts or your iPhone; you don't notice these old relics and can't imagine the beauty and the stories that lie behind their closed doors. It's the little signs of life when we visit these uninhabited buildings that I particularly love, the scribbles on the walls from people adding things up,

measuring things, or just little notes, the signs of humanity etched into the building.

Ben: Yes, I love those, too, it's like those bits of the empty building are its scars, its stretch marks, its tattoos – they're the bits that hint at the lives it held. I love the way people leave their mark on the city. It's such a privilege that we get to witness and record them before they go. Because even if a building is listed, those details are often lost in the restoration process.

Natasha: It reminds you – getting a bit deep! – but it reminds you of your own mortality. It's so easy to go through day after day after day, busy, busy, busy and not stop to think…

Ben: …you'll be dead one day!

Natasha: Well, yeah! And the people who did exist in those buildings, who turned those doorknobs, painted with those brushes, are gone, so just to stop and look at that, even briefly, is humbling and somehow gives you a sense of who you are now. Do you remember the sculptor's studio in the mannequin factory? Here's this tiny room, where one man spent most of his life hidden away from the city with these beautiful models who would come in. He painted them, sketched them, worked away making their casts and moulds –

that's what's striking to me. That this city is so big and there are all these undiscovered corners.

Ben: Yeah…and the beauty of these places reminds me of a wider one. You peer into these hidden corners, but even as you're appreciating these, soon to be gone, corners that have been closed off to you, you have a better appreciation of all the nooks and crannies in London and of all these undiscovered lives being led right now behind the walls of buildings across the city.

ROBERT LORDAN

WINDOWS TO THE PAST

What I love about London are its subtle hints of the past, the long defunct parts which manage to hang on, sitting quietly by while all else evolves at a hectic pace.

These reminders reach all the way back to Roman times, the clearest example being the old city wall which can still be appreciated in substantial chunks around the historic Square Mile. Some parts pop up in unexpected places – peer through the window of Towergate Insurance on Leadenhall Street near Aldgate junction and you'll see part of the wall inside, incorporated into the office.

To see more of Londinium pop into the basement of the Guildhall Gallery, where you'll find the remains of the city's amphitheatre: a sombre reminder of that era's brutality.

There are other telling walls, too. The peaceful St George's Garden in Borough, for instance, is home to a dark, imposing wall which is the only remaining portion of the old Marshalsea Prison, the very jail in which Charles Dickens's father was incarcerated for debt. In Wapping, you can marvel at the hefty towering brickwork which once guarded the city's lucrative docks from thieves and pirates.

Transport has always been intrinsic to London's development, but as the city has grown certain parts of its infrastructure have fallen out of use. The most obvious of these are London Underground's numerous "ghost stations", such as Aldwych, York Road and Down Street: unassuming buildings tiled in oxblood red, perched above the gusty tunnels that echo far below.

On Kingsway, near Holborn, an old tram tunnel can be seen sloping deep into the ground, while a little further out from the centre, the East Cross Route and elevated Westway hint at ambitious 1960s road schemes that were never fully realised.

BLACK CABBIE AND **AWARD-WINNING BLOGGER**

Canals once played an important part in London's development too and the old waterways remain, tucked away from Little Venice to Hackney, where they offer an oasis of calm. More unusual is the old Surrey Quays Canal, which has long since been filled in but can still be traced via roads and bridges from Rotherhithe to Camberwell.

London has many other "lost" waterways: little branches of the Thames now channelled beneath the ground, such as the Effra, the route of which is marked by a road through Brixton, while the sloping banks of the Fleet are still evident at Ludgate Circus. In the summer, the smell of the Fleet sometimes drifts up through the drains – a pungent whiff of old London.

War has also shaped London, and crater-like scars can be seen on some buildings such as the Victoria & Albert Museum and St Clement Danes Church. Elsewhere, it is still possible to see painted signs pointing towards long-vanished air-raid shelters. More curious are the sturdy, metal stretchers stockpiled to carry those injured in the Blitz, but which have since been converted into innovative fencing panels visible outside several old council estates.

Some glimpses of the past are grand but overlooked, such as Holborn's Staple Inn, a timber-framed Tudor building which provides a rare glimpse of London's pre-Great Fire character.

Another example is the mighty clock tower in Caledonian Park, once the centrepiece of the Metropolitan Cattle Market. Further south is Crystal Palace Park, where the famous glass palace once stood, the area now dotted with leftover sphinxes and other statues, as well as the charming dinosaur park which provides an intriguing view of how the Victorians envisioned prehistoric times.

There are little reminders of old London everywhere and if you keep your eyes open, discovering these windows to the past can be a true joy.

BIBI LYNCH

BAR BRUNO, SOHO

There are two rituals associated with my Soho Radio show: a ceremonious "earrings off and Vaseline on" (don't) just before we go on air – and a wired post-show visit to the wonderful Bar Bruno on Wardour Street. Me and my producer – the fortuitously named Producer Nick – turn up *minutes* after the show ends. We *rush* to get there; we love it so much.

It's not just the fabulous fry-ups (I always have egg, bacon, mushrooms and chips – and steal a slice of Producer Nick's thick white-bread toast) – but the place, the feel, the people.

I love the plastic "holed" flooring behind the counter that my heels always catch in as I make my way down the stairs to the loo behind the storeroom.

I love the feisty, funny waitress Iwona with the barbed-wire tattoo who calls me "Bella" and has never once judged my decaf requests.

I love that Bruno's Breakfast ("BB") is almost my name. (I know.)

I love the ceiling-to-floor black-and-white photo collages on the walls, depicting Soho memories good and bad… "Girls, Girls, Girls"; naughty drunken revellers; Soho residents from forever ago; shocked victims gasping outside the bombed Admiral Duncan pub…

I love how Bar Bruno is Soho. Old-school Soho – but today's Soho, too. It beautifully represents London's greatest square mile: warm and welcoming, inclusive, unimpressed ("Your play's on over the road? Bravo. Now pass the vinegar."), full of characters, makes you smile and is the right side of cheap.

Bar Bruno *is* Soho in the most magical sense, too – somehow giving you that feeling of attachment and belonging in a huge, international city. How? I don't know. I'm just some bird who turns up, eats the great food, enjoys the fantastic company, soaks up the brilliant atmosphere, and leaves smelling of chips. I love it.

JOURNALIST, COLUMNIST, WRITER AND **BROADCASTER** ON **SOHO FM**

ANNE MANINGAS

LONDON'S TUBE

I was about five or maybe six, and I distinctly remember the spectacle of being half caught and half smacked in the face by the paddles of the ticket barriers at Hammersmith Station; I had been distracted by the sound and the feel of a Piccadilly Line train passing under my feet and had hesitated while passing through the gates, trying to follow my mother, who was now shrieking over the squealing noise of the barriers.

I was quickly freed from the Underground's grasp. But the release from its hold would not last long. It never does, does it? People make this city: our tunnel infrastructure supports it; our trains breathe life into it by transporting us from A to B. I have seen break-ups on station platforms. I have seen reunions on staircases. I have seen chance meetings between long-lost friends in ticket halls during the morning rush hour. From the station platforms at Stratford, we saw our London grow to play host to the world.

When I started working at North Greenwich Station when I was 18, I could see that London's subterranean railway also ran on parents handing over their children to the grandparents in the mornings, as they embarked on another day earning their keep in the City. Our great city, with underground trains running through its tunnel-like veins. Now I am nearly 28 and, as a train driver on the Metropolitan Railway, I can tell you that on some early mornings my soul feeds on the first light and the dawn drenching the tops of the rails in Uxbridge sidings, as well as the evening twilight that comes to hug the fringes of London.

The fading light falls on our faces on the commute home, with the smell of train brake dust lingering, edged with a soundtrack of whooshing sliding doors and faint public announcements. I discovered at a very young age that London life is a cacophony of fleeting moments, with the Underground as a backdrop for it all. The older I got, the more intrigued I became, and this curiosity and wonder about the Underground soon became an obsession. There is something about our wonderful subterranean railway that grips me on a daily basis; I'm not sure whether it's the lure of Edward Johnston's famous typeface; or whether it's the colours or the sounds. Or it may be the small experiences of life that are sampled along corridors and passageways, spiced with the echoes of a busker and his guitar.

All I know is that the various Tube lines are inextricably intertwined with life here in London. And so, when a much senior colleague said to me, "Listen here, lass – this railway runs on tea and gossip," you can imagine the look I must've given him.

LONDON UNDERGROUND TRAIN DRIVER
AND **PHOTOGRAPHER**

Roger Mavity

Business expert, bestselling author and trustee of the Photographer's Gallery

HALF AN HOUR IN ANOTHER TIME – A WALK UP ST JAMES'S STREET

When I first came to London I was 18, and broke. I walked everywhere, not because I preferred to, but because it was free. But what started as a need quickly became a pleasure. I've always found walking in the country rather boring: one field looks much like any other to me. But walking in a city is different. Excitement and surprise lie in wait round every corner. My first London walk was back from my office in seedy Paddington to my tiny flat in Gloucester Road. It began with depressing cheap hotels on all sides; then suddenly I was in the gracious green of Hyde Park; and then the white stucco elegance of Kensington. Later, I found a less microscopic flat off the King's Road and a girlfriend in Pimlico. I'd stay in her flat till the early hours and then walk home past the unaffordably magnificent antique shops of Pimlico Road and down the buzz of the King's Road.

But my favourite London walk is to go up St James's Street. In the first 200 metres you've gone back 200 years.

Start at the bottom, where Pall Mall turns into St James's Street and go up the hill, hugging the east side. You pass Berry Brothers & Rudd, surely the most distinguished wine merchant you could imagine. Go inside and soak up an atmosphere which hasn't changed since Dickens's time. So that you don't feel guilty about window-shopping, buy a bottle of their Good Ordinary Claret (and it is good, though not that ordinary in my view). Then you pass Lobb,

the fabulous (and fabulously pricey) makers of traditional handmade shoes. Next is Lock & Co., the equally ancient hatters. Go in and buy a Panama for your next holiday and soak up another historic experience. You are now deep in English gentleman territory, so you probably ought to wheel into Fox the cigar merchant and treat yourself to a box of Cohiba. If they don't tempt you, there's Davidoff just up the road, an even grander cigar emporium. I once went there to buy one solitary long, thin cigar, as I was going to a fancy-dress party as a Mississippi riverboat gambler. They treated my request with the same seriousness as if I had been a connoisseur buying a box of a hundred Gran Coronas.

You're now on the corner of Jermyn Street. Turn right and wander past all of those splendidly old-fashioned shirtmakers, like Harvie & Hudson and Turnbull & Asser. You'll also pass Trevor Philip, an antique shop which specialises in old globes, exquisite telescopes and the like. At Paxton & Whitfield you will see an unmatchable array of cheeses. If that makes you hungry, cross over Jermyn Street to Wiltons, the most magnificently traditional restaurant in London, and have a bottle of claret with your roast grouse and game chips.

Now walk up one of the elegant arcades that link Jermyn Street to Piccadilly. Suddenly you are returned to the real world of Starbucks, tourists, trainers and backpacks. But you have just had half an hour in the wonderland of the 18th century.

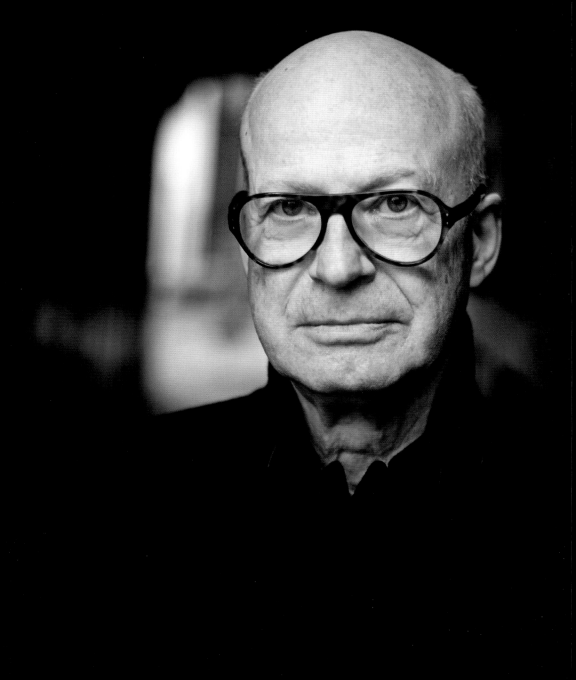

Bill McLachlan

13-year-old schoolboy

—

YOUNG IN LONDON

—

Living in London, something I'm very grateful to be able to say, has left me incredibly spoiled for choice; the sheer number of opportunities open to my friends and me from such young ages blows my mind.

I've been fortunate enough to experience things which really are unique to the young people of London. These stretch from visiting the many fantastic, free museums and art galleries all across the city, to being able to look out of my kitchen window and be met with a view of the Thames, even if it's only a glimpse – these are things that I think Londoners occasionally take for granted.

It's only when you take a second to reflect on these privileges that you realise quite how lucky we are to live in this great city. I don't think that there is a particular thing that attracts me to London. I suppose that being here just kind of leaves me hooked. There's something that makes it very appealing to kids my age and that's most likely down to the sheer variety of work available here on such a large scale. Technology start-ups such as Shazam (an innovative application made in London) fascinate me because to know that in the not-so-far-off future I could, depending on what happens in the next few years…ahem, be working on something as innovative as this, is wildly exciting. With London being the epicentre of tech in the UK, if I were to look for a career in this area then I wouldn't look anywhere other than here.

Will I always live here? I don't know, though I hope I do. Right now I'm just enjoying living here, happy to never really be bored like I might be somewhere where there aren't all of these great opportunities, where there isn't always something to do or to go to. But here, there are all of these things and I wouldn't give them up for a fortune.

TATIANA MERCER

THE BEAUFORT BAR AT THE SAVOY

Although I write about bars, the place I love most in London is actually not really very me, because I'm not the kind of person who drinks £20 cocktails, even though it's my job to do that. It's the Beaufort Bar at the Savoy. They closed it for years to renovate it. Now you go there and feel like you probably shouldn't be allowed in, but at the same time you can take your mother, your grandmother, your boyfriend, your hipster friend – and they'll all love it there.

It is so British and so London, but it's also incredibly welcoming, whereas other places aren't so inviting. You go in and you're greeted by the guy in the hat. There's the American Bar when you walk in, which is where some of the most classic cocktails were created, but it's the Beaufort I like. If you go through further into the building you'll find it. It's the most beautiful bar: it's got a stupid amount of gold leaf on the wall; the whole thing is gold. They have live music – Elton John has played there. You feel like you have been taken back to the *Titanic* era, you just feel so special. The service is amazing, the drinks are incredible. It's a unique place.

I write about cocktails, but I can't actually make them. The female bartender at the Beaufort said she'd teach me how to make a Manhattan. She taught me everything I needed to know. It was just the most amazing experience. The next time I went there with a friend, Duran Duran were shooting a video and we were told, "You guys can be in it if you want." I don't think we made the cut – there were all the biggest supermodels in the world there, and then just us, sitting there having a drink.

My husband and I went there on our first date and they showed us the best time – we were given a glass of champagne on arrival, so that's probably another reason why I have fond memories of the place.

If I had to recommend a drink to try at the Beaufort, it would probably be an Old Fashioned or a Martini, but I'm quite a flexible drinker. That's the great thing about it: the service is so great there, you can go knowing nothing or knowing everything about drinks. You can just say you like vodka and would like something sweet and you'll get a world-class drink. I don't normally like champagne but if you're going to drink it, it tastes especially good there.

The Beaufort Bar really does make me proud of London. There are loads of amazing places in this city, but you really can't recreate history. You can try, but you just can't do it if you don't have the foundation.

FOUNDER OF BARCHICK.COM

GILES MILLER

STUDIO IN SPITALFIELDS

London for me is a day in the small design studio I run in Spitalfields, starting with the journey down Bow Road towards the City. Norman Foster's Gherkin and the new Leadenhall Building by Richard Rogers are visible for almost the entire length of the journey, and all the way down Whitechapel Road the architecture of the city lures you. Imagine having two towering achievements of British architecture so near; how wonderful to be able to gaze at them with half an eye as I scoot to work every day.

If I arrive early enough, I often have the pleasure of a knowing look and perhaps even an acknowledging raise of the eyebrow from none other than Gilbert Prousch and George Passmore, otherwise known as British artist duo Gilbert and George. These two gentlemen, always impeccably dressed in tweed and formidable headwear, walk past our door every day as they maintain their ever-consistent route around the East End. These chaps won the Turner Prize in 1986, when I was three years old.

Around the back of our block you will find the studio of none other than Tracey Emin, renowned British artist who once formed part of the YBAs and whose work won her a Turner Prize nomination in 1999. Emin is a hugely talented and very influential international artist. Her studio is enormous, and her presence is felt all around Spitalfields, in places such as the Golden Heart pub, with its fluorescent lighting installations.

We are leaving Spitalfields soon, and we need to make the most of all this genius. I've promised £100 to the first person to bring Tracey, Gilbert or George into our studio for a cup of tea.

AWARD-WINNING **ARCHITECTURAL DESIGNER**

Shirley Murgraff

East Londoner and lifelong campaigner

VICTORIA PARK

Born in 1931, the seventh of eight children, I grew up opposite Lauriston Road School, South Hackney. The small parade of shops offered a range of evocative aromas: the Italian cafe's ice cream and boiling spaghetti, the tailor's steaming cloth, our glorious roasting coffee beans and fresh-ground coffee, cigarette smoke – quite different from my father's Player's – from the Turkish tobacconist who favoured waxed moustaches, gleaming black oiled hair and spats, and the enticing warm air rising from the pavement grill of the bakery which is still there.

A good deal of the area was very poor: I remember the undernourished kids in my infants' class (school milk notwithstanding) with permanent colds and holes in their jumpers. Now, the attractive 1891 school building houses astronomically priced luxury flats (a two-bed apartment advertised for £1.625 million!) and the whole place is called "The Village". Go figure.

Barely five minutes away was wonderful Victoria Park, with its magnificent wrought-iron gates and entirely surrounded by glistening high railings (removed for "the war effort" and never replaced, probably still rusting at the bottom of the English Channel).

My adored father worked all hours, and our rare and precious time with him was our Saturday afternoon walks in the park. To me aged five it was, unfailingly, an almost magical place. The aviary with its exotic birds seemed huge. The beautifully tended "old English garden" was a feast of colour, scents and intriguing geometrical patterns in the formal flowerbeds – all dug up in 1940 for air-raid

shelters. I remember the searchlights and the huge anti-aircraft batteries which, during air raids, rained down shrapnel over a wide area.

The wallabies in their rocky enclosure played endearingly, the small deer grazed unthreateningly – unlike the occasional barking dogs – and of course there was the duck pond, whose occupants appeared able to consume unending supplies of stale bread without ill effect. Over it all reigned the Park Rangers – "Parkies" – in their brown uniforms complete with waistcoats. As long as you behaved they kept a friendly order throughout, and ensured compliance with the posted instruction "Please leave the park when the bell is rung", which occurred 30 minutes before closing time.

On the other side were the swings, slide and roundabout, with the attendant supervisor who cut short any abuse of the drinking fountain; the often empty tennis courts; more tall trees, and green open spaces with the unfamiliar smell of new-cut grass (we had back yards, not gardens, so we revelled in the space). There was the serene boating lake with its earnest, unpractised rowers, whose concentration was regrettably interrupted by the loudhailer calling, "Time's up, come in number 7!" And, at the end, the mixed-emotion thrill of crossing the canal by the wooden bridge – clinging tight to my father's hand for fear of falling between the slats – to get to the "pagoda".

Treasured memories of times which all ended suddenly with evacuation in September 1939, after which, because of his untimely death in 1942, I never saw my father again.

SCARLETT NASH

LEAVING LONDON FOR THE LAST TIME

With the work I do, I am fortunate enough to be exposed to every personality, nook and cranny that dear old London town has to offer. Not knowing what story is situated behind each door and, more importantly, whose story.

We regard life as precious but unpredictable and this feeling is evoked through the people we care for who are born and raised Londoners and have some incredible stories to tell. Some of which you will never have the pleasure of reading or watching in the cinema. Stories precious and unique to those individuals, their memories of London shared with us and given to us absolutely free!

From 28-year-old Jess telling us about the time she ended up singing "Hit the road, Jack" with a busker at Brixton Station at one o'clock one Monday morning, earning herself £2.75, to 96-year-old Kenneth telling us about his first kiss with Denise on the summit of Hampstead Heath in 1921. We keep in touch with Denise who to this day still visits "their spot" every second Wednesday, to reminisce on all their years together, repeating their memories in her mind.

The story that stood out the most was from 98-year-old Harry, who had been with his partner Albert for almost 70 years. He spoke to us about the trials they faced most of their lives, being in a secret relationship, often quoting, "I'll tell you this now, human beings absolutely stink – you'll pinch your nose with some of it!" But Harry felt this never hindered their love for one another. He went on to speak about the evolving acceptance of this in London, then its spread through the UK and, to his astonishment, some of the rest of the world. He felt that in his later years, London became his colourful and spirited safe haven where he could walk freely or, as he liked to say, "hobble on the cobbles" through London. Harry explained that instead of bearing witness to shrugging looks he and Albert were now given gentle, judgement-free smiles instead. This is why Harry loved London and we are so grateful to him for sharing this with us, as speaking about it brought many tears to his eyes, lifting some very difficult memories right back to the surface.

With this we'd like to say thank you to Jess, Kenneth and Harry and to all of those special people we have the pleasure to meet who shared their love of London with us. Thank you all, you will all be well remembered and greatly missed.

RIP Jess, Kenneth, Harry and Albert.

Best wishes to Denise.

COMMUNITY **PALLIATIVE CARE**
NURSE, ROYAL TRINITY HOSPICE

RUPERT NEWMAN

LONDON AS A CANVAS

I use light as a medium to transform architecture, both old and new. The buildings of London are full of contrast, reflecting its long history of growth and development. From illuminating the 19th-century altar of One Mayfair to the interior of a sophisticated penthouse overlooking the River Thames; from the glamorous ballroom at the Savoy Hotel to the decaying interior of the original iconic Battersea Power Station; from the facade of the medieval Guildhall to the London Business School, designed by John Nash, London offers an extremely diverse range of canvases upon which I can project my unique visual imprint, and thus momentarily transform small corners of this inspirational city.

It was during a show in Soho that my illuminations really caught the attention of an onlooker. The altar in the intimate Chapel of the House of St Barnabas was my canvas. Accompanied by choral music, multicoloured prismatic structures shattered and realigned, creating powerful illusions and effects that danced around the central crucifix. The centrality of Jesus to the experience was impossible to escape, and the existing religious sensibility of the space was intensified. It all became a bit much for one onlooker who began to dance around in circles, as if rejoicing. I stood back for a minute before approaching her. Maybe it's some sort of mystical experience, I thought. Has she seen the light?! "Is everything okay?" I asked. I noticed the mobile phone she held was flashing. "Yes! My daughter's just got engaged!"

LIGHT PROJECTION ARTIST

DAVID NOTT

BEATING THE TRAFFIC BY BICYCLE

Most of my time I zip around London on my pushbike. I've lived in London for over 20 years, and I've always cycled around the city. I cycle everywhere, mostly from home to work, which is three hospitals: Chelsea and Westminster, St Mary's Paddington and the Royal Marsden.

I do have a motorbike, for when I need to whiz from home to a real emergency. When I'm at Chelsea and Westminster, I'm a general surgeon; when I'm at St Mary's, I'm a vascular and trauma surgeon. I live just below Imperial Wharf in Fulham, so I'm not far from any of the three hospitals. If I get called to respond to, for example, a stabbing in the chest or heart – which I did during the Notting Hill Carnival this year – I just whiz through traffic.

You really can get from A to B as fast as possible on a bike. You always know you can get to where you're headed without being held up. It's very unusual that I'm late for anything, whereas in a car you never know where the roadworks are, you're never on time…

Over the years I've lived in London, I'd say that cycling has become both easier and harder in the city: easier because of the blue cycle lanes; harder because there is more traffic and also because I try to stick to the road-safety guidelines, but some cyclists fly through red lights and make it more difficult for all of us. The traffic is much more intense today than it was ten to fifteen years ago; it's much worse, and there's much more likelihood of big lorries not seeing you.

Amazingly, I've been knocked off my motorbike twice but I haven't been knocked off my bicycle at all. I cycle through London traffic between five and ten miles every day. I think you just have to be very savvy.

Most of the time when I'm on my bike I listen to Radio 4 *Today*, and when I'm seriously happy I'll listen to some rock music, usually on my way home. One of my most enjoyable things is to go between the traffic at high speed on my bike when it's all completely gridlocked; I'll be whizzing through, listening to rock.

The best route for me is through Hyde Park. Travelling to St Mary's Hospital through the park in the autumn time is one of the nicest routes. You see the beauty of London over the Serpentine. The view from there is incredible.

Sometimes, when it's early morning, you can see this low-level mist over Hyde Park and it's so beautiful and atmospheric. There's no one around at that sort of time, which makes it more special. At dusk, when I'm cycling home after a really hard day at the hospital, there's nothing better than freewheeling down the road with the wind in my hair. I find it a great calming influence riding a bicycle through London. I'd hate to be penned in on the Tube. It's much more liberating being on a bicycle.

WAR **SURGEON** AND **CONSULTANT** TO THREE **LONDON HOSPITALS**

John Pearse

Tailor and founder of seminal King's Road shop Granny Takes a Trip

TODAY

It's my great pleasure cycling through Hyde Park in the morning.

A London war baby conceived just blocks away.

At Speakers' Corner, "Hail The King", aka Dave. Stately African, grey-bearded, deep in conversation with himself.

Army greatcoat, pointed beany, a jaunty elegance that sometimes comes with being destitute. We exchange greetings. I give alms, receive benediction.

Onwards via the tunnel under Park Lane.

More homeless in sleeping bags line the route. Sometimes gypsy violins, metal guitar, Mozart flute create ambience. Drop coins, emerge.

Shepherd Market. Now clean of vice, filthy with lucre…

Hedge funders take discreet breakfast meetings on the terrace of Loulou's exclusive club named after Yves Saint Laurent's muse whose first brief wedding I recall at the Ritz. Now she's gone. So many memories…

Minutes later, J P Soho Tailor's establishment. Meard Street. Church-bell chimes, birdsong upon the roof, life's as rural as can be in the heart of the city.

Once a modish youth hung out, savouring all nightlife on offer. Another story.

Granny's World's End made sartorial impact on King's Road back in the day…

The parade of stoned harlequins, Hippy Trippy dogma, soon bored J P.

Life switched to Rome and a passion for cinema. Fellini, Godard, Warhol inspired him to create superstars and film his beloved London. BLACK AND WHITE '60S REQUIEM…

TEMPUS FUGIT.

The MOVIE reels on in COLOUR, 2016.

EXT.138 PARK LANE. DAY, VOICE-OVER ON SOUNDTRACK. CAMERA SLOWLY ZOOMS IN, CARESSING THE BUILDING.

The VOICE is sexy and seductive; it belongs to a MAYFAIR MERC estate agent. She's well versed in dealing in high numbers.

THE CAMERA CONTINUES making love to the BUILDING…

VOICE-OVER

Newly restored in Mayfair. The Grade II-listed building has been granted a new luxurious lease of life under the watchful eye of English Heritage.

Built in 1832, it overlooks Marble Arch and was given a completely new look in the early 20th century by the great British architect Sir Edwin Lutyens.

This location is perfect for those who wish to entertain and shop in nearby designer boutiques… EXT. 138 PARK LANE. SHOT FROM THE ROOF, DAWN.

The first grey light of DAWN. All is quiet in the sleeping city. All is…

Eeeyahmmaheeyahmmmmmaheeyeh. The shrill nasal Muslim whine shatters the dawn quiet…

AN ARAB on the BALCONY kneels on his prayer mat, making his obeisance to Mecca.

CUT TO

EXT. EDGWARE ROAD PAVEMENT CAFE, DUSK.

J P wreathed in smoke from his shisha pipe. Yet another exotic parade goes by.

He gradually DISSOLVES into the smoke…

FADE OUT

JO PHILLIPS

MY FIRST LONDON COFFEE

My Dad was in the rag trade, albeit the high end of it, but nevertheless what would be called in Yiddish the *schmatte* trade.

His factory was off the Old Kent Road and many a Saturday was spent in the dusty expanse of an industrial unit at the very unglamorous end of Southeast London.

Twice a year, however, things changed and became a little more upmarket. During the biannual selling season, Saturdays were often spent "up West" in the showroom in the fashion district all around Eastcastle Street (where my Dad's showroom was), and where the buying and selling of said *schmatte* took place.

One such Saturday I will never forget because it was one of those "coming of age" moments. Not a big slushy Hollywood-style affair, but one of those little moments when a parent passes on some nugget of the adult world to a not-quite-teenage child but one on the cusp.

My Dad loved all things Italian: food, clothes, shoes and of course coffee. At that point (mid-1970s), the West End was dotted with Italian-style coffee shops. I can't have been older than ten, but Dad took my sister and me for our first real Italian coffee. We sat on a side street at a little table of a coffee bar and he ordered us all coffee, black, with cream on the side. I clearly remember him showing me how to put in the sugar properly, stir it and then pour cream over a turned-over spoon in order to get a really thick, sweet, creamy top to truly dark, rich coffee.

It never turned me into a big coffee drinker, but I can't drink a cup of coffee, whether it be something horrid freeze-dried from a jar or a freshly brewed ground-beans mixture, without thinking of that day.

Up West, with my Dad, drinking coffee at a pavement bar. Magic.

CREATIVE DIRECTOR OF CENT MAGAZINE

Grace Pilkington

Journalist and poet

—

MY BUSH

—

I tried most things for the first time on the Goldhawk Road. My first breath was at Queen Charlotte's Hospital, my first bike ride was in Ravenscourt Park, my first cigarette was between the Biffa bins in the alleyway next to Sports Direct, and the first and only time I was beaten up was outside Rajput. I would like to be able to say I had sex for the first time outside the market, but it was in Chelsea (you've really made it when you're sleeping with someone who lives on the 49 bus route). I was first offered drugs outside Goldhawk Road Station. A man asked if I was waiting for Ian and when I replied that I was waiting for my Dad, he asked if my Dad wanted any gear. Shepherd's Bush is the most hideous and the most beautiful place in the world, in the most exhilarating city in the world.

I spent my childhood with the Circle Line; the school journey meant a race down the carriages and a swing on the monkey bars/handrails. Weekends involved chugging around the yellow Tube line with a bottle of Hooch. We would sit on the railings outside McDonald's or the town hall like pigeons in the hope that among us we might have enough for a milkshake.

I soon ditched the Circle Line: I wanted something faster, more underground and exciting. The Central Line rocketed me to Shoreditch, where I wore a pork-pie hat, drank Cosmopolitans out of jam jars, ate eel and talked art.

My next fling was with the Victoria Line: we met in Brixton and it took me to Bloomsbury, where I worked in a maze of books and toured Charlotte Street for lunches.

I'm now with the Jubilee Line, a line I've always quite fancied, and when I board on Shoot-Up Hill there's a lot of London it still has up its sleeve.

But my favourite way to spend a day is back on the Shepherd's Bush roundabout, trying out all the different worlds it offers. I can see Lady Antonia Fraser munch a Lidgate pie in Holland Park, or suave my way to Kensington. Or I can bang on the doors of the recently closed Duke of Edinburgh pub where the sign reads "NO I.O.Us" and "Bring your own ice". I can cover myself in the Goldhawk Road's flowing fluorescent fabrics or go gothic at a Metallica gig in the Empire. I can follow a trolley filled with raw meats through the market and munch the finest kebab, or I can globetrot from North Pole Road to South Africa Road and see the Rs: my team, Queen's Park Rangers. If I wanted a panic attack I could pop into Westfield or, if I was sporty, I could play a game of five-a-side under the Westway. I could even hit the A40 and leave altogether. But why the hell would I want to do that?

Because even when I feel as if I've been churned up and spat out like an old can of Lilt by the Thames, I'm still glad it was the Thames that spat me out.

Kate Poland

Guerilla gardener

—

LONDON'S GARDENING OPPORTUNITIES

—

Londoners are opportunists. We have to be. We are competing with each other (and nature) for precious space – on transport, in the street, in parks and on any scrap of land not yet claimed. Guerrilla gardeners are arch opportunists, arch Londoners. They see a space – overlooked, unused or abused – and want to make it better by planting something, legitimately or otherwise. They are the pop-up property developers of the plant world.

My first attempt at guerrilla gardening did not go well. An old Jaguar had been left to rust for years in my street and as there was no sign of it moving I thought I'd plant it up and allow nature, as it does, to claim it. What I didn't realise was that there was someone living in the car. And they, quite understandably, didn't want to be greened up.

My second go was on a swathe of land that I could see from my bedroom – a sad, dog- and drunk-marred stretch of grass and brambles. This attempt at getting nature in its greater variety to take hold – with the help of neighbours – *did* work. We even have loose permission to be there (guerrilla lite). We now have allotments, beehives, a pond (and frogs), a shed built from found materials (something else Londoners are good at: "finding" things), dye and herb beds, as well as areas left for wildlife to do what it wants undisturbed.

Guerrilla gardeners need to be armed, of course, and our pockets are full of seeds filched from gardens and walks, ready to fire. We also make our own weapons – balls of clay enclosing seeds in compost, known as seed bombs, which we can lob onto earth we can't get at. I was recently planning a visit to a school to make seed bombs with the children and the teacher said, "Could we

call them something else, something less violent?" We call them seed balls now but a new generation is, hopefully, eyeing up patches of bare soil.

Recently we started counting the number of wild plants growing in the garden – that is, not planted by us but self-seeded, brought in on the bottom of a shoe, in a plant pot, in our hair, by the wind or by birds and other animals. In an hour or so we found 72 varieties. More and more, I see these wild plants as the true Londoners, the true opportunists – the guerrillas. There is a story about London ragwort, the bright yellow daisy-like flower you see along railway tracks in the summer. It was brought to Oxford from Mount Etna by plant hunters and put in the botanic garden there. "Seeing" its opportunity, it started to move, helped by the wind, over the wall and eventually to the railway station. (I've just checked the Botanic Garden's website and they say it's a 20-minute walk but it took about 100 years, so Triffids need not worry us.) Once it got to the tracks (clinker is not unlike volcanic rock), it migrated, like so many of us, to London, where it hybridised and became our own version which thrives in the warmer climate and conditions here. It's made itself at home and is a cheerful addition to our wild flora. (It is also, incidentally, a great favourite of scores of beneficial insects.)

I love seeing the plants we put in our garden wilding themselves and moving on to the next opportunity, seeding in the cracks in the pavement and the mortar in the walls. Only yesterday I saw some sort of kale making its way towards the gate and the world beyond – like the rest of us, taking advantage of the precious space around us.

Jemima Daisy Proudfoot

Wildling writer

—

THE UNDERGROUND ESTABLISHMENT OF STRUGGLING ARTISTS

—

We come here to learn, to create, to be part of this collective culture. We come here because we're not built for the bubbles we were born into. Our intensity outweighs the need for safety. We find ourselves here when nothing else will do. We are all power-walking in the direction of our dreams, consulting Citymapper as we go.

I came to London on a whim. I dropped out of university and gave away all I owned. I packed my bags and left the familiar. Four months in, I was working 90 hours a week, still penniless and exhausted. I was a hamster on a wheel, running with the little energy I had to a destination unknown. If I stood still for only a moment, I was sure this city would relieve me of my sanity.

The reality of London is anything but poetic. The air is filthy and the rent is iniquitous. Outsiders gush at how glamorous it must be to live in the capital; they are unaware of the Northern Line. London is lonely, disparaging and inhospitable, but not once did I question my decision.

We flock here, millions of us, to turn our passion into purpose. We spend our days paying our rent, and our nights as artists. That is, when we're not on yet another Tinder date. Some don't make it, whatever "making it" means. If you're not going at your dreams with full force, London will swallow you whole.

One year in, this is my home. London is ruthless; it slams you to the ground and demands you come up stronger. It gives you nothing and expects everything. But it sets your passions afire, with a constant source of inspiration and opportunity. It is expensive, overpopulated and unforgiving – but this is our city, for better or for worse. We are as passionate about London as we are about our work: the two go hand in hand. Being a Londoner isn't an origin, it is a feeling; no matter where we originated from, this is our home.

Heydon Prowse

Actor, activist, journalist, satirist and comedian

—

Jolyon Rubinstein

Actor, activist, writer, producer and director

—

CONNAUGHT SQUARE

—

Connaught Square is a picturesque square with a private park just off Edgware Road where a number of excellent Middle Eastern restaurants can be found thanks to the large Iraqi population that lives there. Strangely this is also the place Tony Blair chose to make his home. It was this apparent obliviousness to the intensity of ill feeling towards him for his disastrous "humanitarian intervention" into Iraq that gave us the idea to try to beatify Tony for our BBC satire show *The Revolution Will Be Televised*.

We made a stained-glass window depicting Tony as a saint with a halo surrounded by doves and some small Iraqi children thanking him for saving the Middle East and brought it to his door. When the unwitting maid opened the door and asked us in to the former Prime Minister's home, a wonderfully British scene unfolded in which the police constables at the end of the road fast-walked towards us with their machine guns, as if embarrassed to run in case it caused a scene. The constables even patiently waited as we emerged from the house and measured the stained glass against the window above the door (with the help of a stepladder that Blair's maid helpfully provided). It was only when we were all done that they politely took our details, then let us be on our way. London – where you can sneak into the former Prime Minister's house, have a pleasant chat with a courteous machine-gun-wielding police officer and get yourself a fantastic lamb shawarma, all within the space of 150 metres.

NAZNEEN RAHMAN

OLAFUR ELIASSON'S SUN

On a cold, sharp winter's evening in 2003 I happened to be walking along the South Bank. Again. I had no business being there. It was not on the way to my meeting, for which I was already late. My brain knew I should turn back, but my legs kept walking, and my eyes kept drinking in the always astonishing view: a hotchpotch of history in one blink. My soul was soothed, as ever, by the eternal ebbings and flowings of the mighty Thames. Walking along the South Bank I seem to find myself becoming luckier, brighter, stronger, nicer. New science, new music, new versions of me have all materialised on countless walks along that river bank. Inspired by its melee of different cultural and historical references; its quintessential Londonness.

But the winter of 2003 was special. I found myself on the South Bank more than in any other year. Returning and returning to the Tate Modern's Turbine Hall and the sanctuary of Olafur Eliasson's immense sun, the centrepiece of *The Weather Project*, which left me, at once, breathless and lungful. And always, always, I would walk on suffused with gratitude to be living in a city of such beauty, given freely to us all.

GENETICIST SPECIALISING IN
CANCER RESEARCH

Christopher Ramsay

Investment fund sales manager

PORTALS

I work on St James's Street. A 200-metre hill of grand Georgian facades, almost exclusively the reserve of suited men pacing to meetings and the slightly more placid tourist. One usually looking down and the other usually up. A street with no fewer than five "old boys'" clubs, London's oldest wine merchants, at more than 300 years old, and two cigar shops. A street that gets decked in extra-large bunting and Union Jack banners every time Madj has another party. I work in finance, as most people in this street seem to, and whenever I don't have lunch with a client, I like to walk into Soho.

Up Bond Street, past the glitter of De Beers and Cartier, the fine folds of Alexander McQueen and La Perla, onto Old Burlington Street, past the back of the Royal Academy and Cecconi's, with its glamorous clientele sitting outside on their low, blue-and-cream-striped tables, past Savile Row's immaculate stitchings, past the Burberry lobster that hails its own coffee shop and through the never-ending river of red buses that is Regent Street…

You're then through the portal. Suddenly you're in the tight grid system of Soho. Midday it's a black hole of traffic…idle engines providing the bass line to bustling pavements. Cyclists delivering film reels to the editing studios of Old Compton Street rush past interns buying salad boxes for their bosses at M&C Saatchi. A pop-up fashion shop of Central St Martins Art School graduates fills its window with lace and pleather. When the sun shines, I negotiate Golden Square with its thousands sitting among the tulip beds and its all-weather ping-pong

tables. Then onto Lexington Street with its juice bar and the Dickensian date spot that is Andrew Edmunds restaurant. Pot-holed tarmac gives way to the worn cobbles leading to Berwick Street Market. Builders standing outside Soho's latest development wolf-whistle at passing summer busts. Two couriers with matching geometric tattoos sit outside Flat White, stopping their fixed-wheel bikes from falling with a single finger, as they reload on caffeine. I look to see if the window of Agent Provocateur has changed in the 48 hours since my last venture and almost collide with a publican late for his first froth at the Blue Posts.

I cross Wardour Street and pass a subterranean Pilates class next to the studio where Bowie recorded "Space Oddity". Meanwhile the chefs from the all-you-can-eat Cantonese exchange cigarettes with till girls from the artisan bakery.

Finally through a sticker-clad avenue of lampposts, via an un-disappointingly piss-smelling alleyway, I come to my Japanese canteen on Frith Street. Where today I'll sit and write, on their long yellow counter, and eat my lunch. Big fat udon noodles, simple plates of plaice with butter and steaming baskets, all manned by a skilled moustachioed walrus of a chef. "Come On Eileen" on the radio. Chopsticks and napkins from a shared pot.

On the way home I pass the sex shops, fetish book stores and clubs of Old Compton Street. The gay bars and cafés, which so proudly flanked the recent Gay Pride marches, pass beside me as I make my last call of today's pilgrimage: to a

Lebanese MacGyver. A charming, upright man, who wears two, and sometimes three, gold watches on the outside of his silk shirts. A vast, full-bodied mullet of black ringlets reaches down his back like Jason's fleece, heavy, charcoaled and waxed. I ask him for a home-made baklava and by the time the last mouthful is being swallowed I'm over Regent Street and seconds away from my desk.

Portals everywhere…that's why I love London.

Onjali Q Raúf

Founder and director, Making Herstory; research and fundraising co-ordinator for the Limehouse Project in Tower Hamlets

THE SIR JOHN SOANE MUSEUM

One of the most precious, most beloved aspects of London's character is its hidden stash of gems: gems comprising not priceless, glittering stones but mere bricks and mortar, built upon a single person's vision, dogged perseverance and more often than not a hint of tragedy, all concealed in plain sight to forge a secret only tried and tested Londoners are let in on. Take a wander past the hustle and bustle of the perpetually choked streets of Holborn to the quieter backwaters of Lincoln's Inn Fields, and there, at number 13, you will find yourself standing at the doorway of just such a gem: a gem of such infinite wonders as to leave you breathless for days (or in my case decades) to come.

The home and hearth of a bricklayer's son who went on to become one of the nation's most eccentric architects and the designer of the Bank of England, the Sir John Soane Museum lovingly and instantaneously immerses all who enter it into the mind, moods and obsessions of the genius who was Sir John Soane – and his equally passionate wife, Eliza. Deceptively small from the outside, where two Grecian-robed statues stand guard, every wall, ceiling, nook and cranny heaves with antiquities and artworks, plaques and busts, models of ancient ruins and even the ghostly presence of a 3,000-year-old Pharaonic tomb,

painstakingly brought in from the architectural Meccas of Italy, Greece, China and Egypt, together with a good many towns and cities no longer evident on our world maps.

With pathways lit up by mirrors that take their cue from cleverly placed windows, skylights and glass canopies, this universe unto its own creates an illusion of space and light when common sense dictates there should be none. And much like the great British weather, Soane's maze-like house reflects a character whose mood shifts and changes with every step you take. Summery, light-drenched spaces – such as the sitting room where Eliza took company, or the jaw-dropping central dome under which paintings by Canaletto, Greek marbles and Soane's bust daily sunbathe – are waylaid by sudden twists that force you to confront the darker, more enigmatic side to the man in whose home you wander. From the eerie presence of the Gothic-styled cell (complete with skull) which Soane fashioned for a monk alive solely in his imagination, to the spine-prickling set of slaves' chains that hang like a visual slap in the bare, whitewashed belly of the house, this humble-looking townhouse marries wo/mankind's capacity to create, invent and envision with stark reminders of the cruelties and tragedies that often underlie and overshadow our greatest achievements.

For me, Sir John Soane and his world embody the history of all that has gone into making London – and England – what it is today. It is a gentle reminder that the foundation of this great city is made up of a heady mixture of ideas and ideologies, beauties and inspirations literally shipped in from peoples and lands across the globe to craft the landscape and fast-beating heart of the London we see and love today. But more than anything, it is an open invitation to every person who enters to embark on a journey of their own, to search their own passions, understandings and sense of self, and to leave inspired: an invitation which I, in the manner of a true Londoner, extend, on Soane's behalf, to you.

EMMA RICE

WATERLOO BRIDGE

Without a doubt, my favourite place in London is smack bang in the middle of Waterloo Bridge.

When I first came to London as a student from Nottingham, this was the place where it suddenly all made sense. It wasn't a remote and scary room in Walthamstow, or a crowded smelly Tube train – this was London! I could stand, floating above the water, and turn to see everything I had dreamed of: the National Theatre, the Houses of Parliament, the dome of St Paul's and a small tower that I called the Bone Tower. It looked like delicate vertebrae reaching to the sky and I recognised something in its fragility that struck a chord. I still don't know its name, but it will always be the Bone Tower to me.

Now, almost 30 years on, I still love this place, but perhaps for different reasons. I see and love the changes that time has brought – the London Eye, the Millennium Bridge and also the promise, tucked around the corner of the Thames, of my new home, the Globe. But mostly it is the openness and the call of urban nature that visit me in this place. Waterloo Bridge is now my Cornish cliff-top, my sharp gust of heavenly drizzle and my cool lung. Here, I can breathe, I can see the wonderful, story-filled, chaotic horizon and nothing seems that bad any more. Magic.

ACTOR AND **ARTISTIC DIRECTOR**
OF SHAKESPEARE'S **GLOBE THEATRE**

The Lord Richards of Herstmonceux

Former Chief of the Defence Staff of the British Army

—

KENSINGTON GARDENS

—

One of London's most wonderful features is the parks and green spaces that crop up in so many, often unlikely, places. A carefully planned walk can go for miles with hardly a break from trees and grass. My favourite place is Kensington Gardens. With its grass deliberately left unmanicured and its trees full of birds from rare owls to parakeets, it is delightfully rural, indeed almost a little wild, and for me and my family very special: a place where families play, exotically dressed visitors picnic, strangers safely strike up conversations and eccentric loners practise strange sports. For me it is our cosmopolitan and immensely varied city at its very best and I can never get enough of it.

John Rogers

Writer and film-maker; author of *This Other London: Adventures in the Overlooked City*

THIS OTHER LONDON

When my first son was born he would fall asleep on my shoulder in the hours before first light. The smallest move would wake him. While he slumbered I would occupy myself by randomly flicking through the pages of an A-Z – a whole new exotic world opened up before me, which once the kids were old enough I set out to explore. This other London is where we live – Hounslow, Catford, Higham Hill – born from utopian dreams and an outburst of civic pride, pioneering architects employed to design the Tube stations and the department stores on the high road now hidden behind generic chain-store shop fronts.

One Remembrance Sunday I followed a Neolithic trackway from Charles Holden's modernist Sudbury Hill Station over Horsenden Hill, down through Perivale, then across Scotch Common to Hanwell, where seven Saxon warriors lie buried beneath a cul-de-sac, still clasping spears across their chests, hemp cloaks fastened with elaborately decorated bronze brooches. A local legend talks of the fairy princess Ealine who slumbers under the tarmac of the bus interchange at Haven Green, where you can get cracking fish and chips.

On the other side of town, climbing through Bostall Woods I walked among the medieval ruins of Lesnes Abbey, occupying a high promontory overlooking Plumstead Marshes with views stretching out to Tilbury and beyond. It was excavated in 1753 by the great antiquarian and druid William Stukeley, who lies buried in the 12th-century church at East Ham. Inhaling, I swore I could smell the sea, although somebody suggested it could be the sewage works at Crossness Point.

Back in the northwest, Cricklewood was once the centre of Britain's aerospace industry. Film studios gravitated to the buzz emanating from the North Circular Road and grand historic epics were produced where today a Matalan with an unusually large carpark stands. Cricklewood lacked the Hollywood chutzpah to spell its name across Dudden Hill, and now its glamorous past is forgotten, a punchline to a smartass joke, the centre of a Year Zero development scheme.

In the 1920s London Transport advertised excursions to places such as Perivale in the way commuters are now enticed to Dubai and Costa Rica. In my youth I went searching for adventure in Sarawak and Rajasthan, but ultimately found it on the Erith salt marshes and in the footprint of the tower blocks at Ponders End, slowly blinking out their last lights before the inevitable estate regeneration shuts them off for good.

To love this "other" London requires an investment in the form of imagination, an Oyster card and a comfortable pair of walking shoes, but once you've clambered up the Norwood Ridge or heard the buried Philly Brook gurgling up from Leytonstone street irons you won't look at Piccadilly Circus or Notting Hill in the same way again.

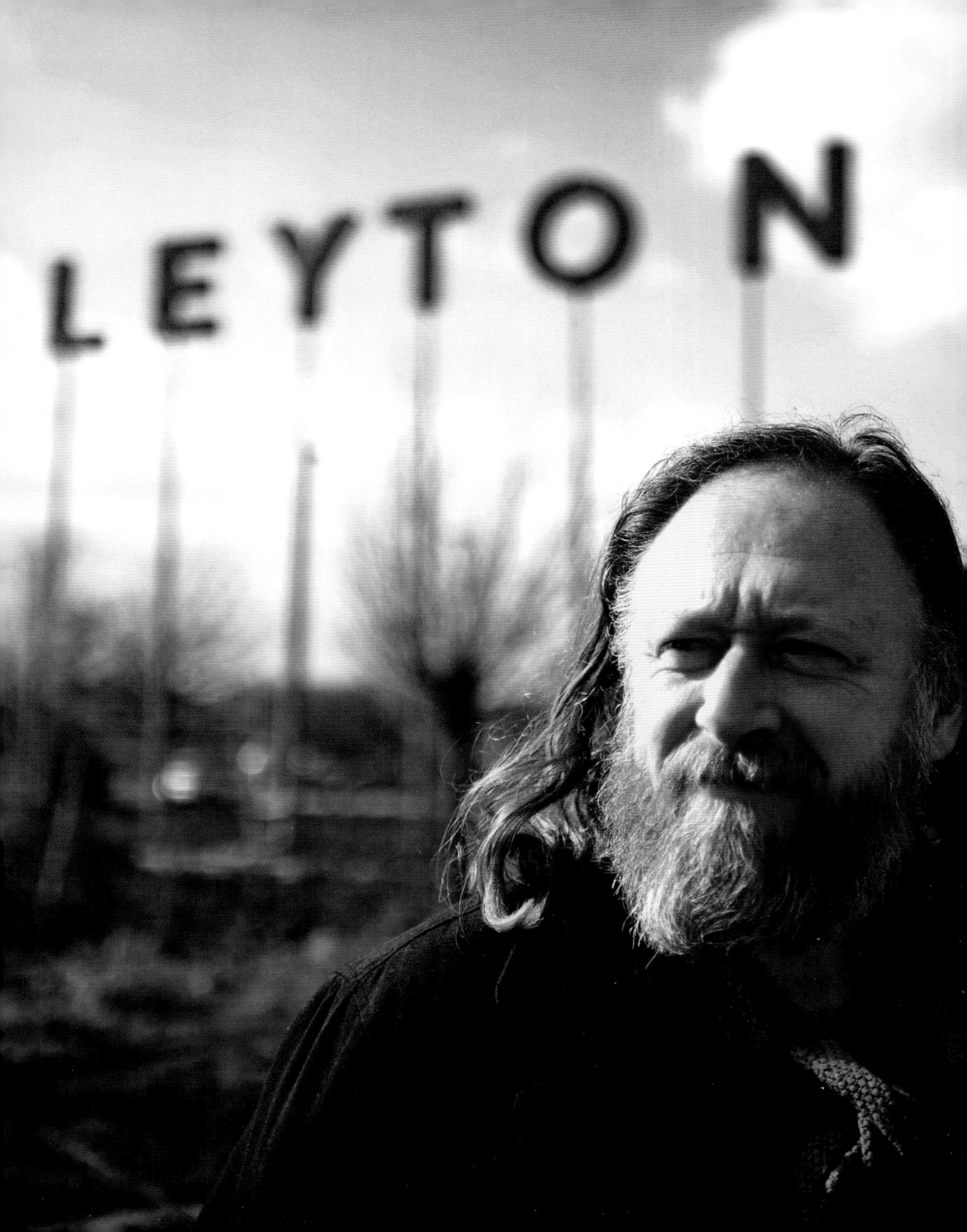
LEYTON

RUTH ROGERS

A CITY OF MANY INGREDIENTS

When I came to London in 1969 you were either British or you were a "foreigner".

In the ensuing years that changed completely.

Britain and the people who lived here became more international – maybe it was the possibility of cheap flights, everyone travelling and exploring and eating such diverse cuisines.

After the publication of our first cookbook, [my partner] Rose and I travelled the country to promote it and the main question was always, "We love your recipes but where can we buy the ingredients?" Today farmers are growing more interesting vegetables; small delis, local markets and supermarkets are interested in organic produce; and the access the Internet gives us has seen cooking and eating change so much for the better.

For me, one of the most exciting things that have happened in the time I've been here in London is that it has become a city of such multiculturalism. Whether I am out having dinner or having a meeting, I look at where people around me have come from and it's so diverse; they have come from so many different countries.

As a chef, watching the process of London becoming a multicultural city has meant witnessing incredible progress. Even olive oil, which today everyone has in their kitchen, you couldn't get hold of readily when I first arrived in London. Yet now we have so many different types of olive oil and so many outlets to buy it from.

When you have access and choice the cooking becomes more exciting, more sustainable – and delicious.

CHEF AND PROPRIETOR OF THE **RIVER CAFÉ**

Ekaterina Rozenbaum

Lawyer

FALLING IN LOVE WITH LONDON

Do you believe in love at first sight? I do – it's how I felt when I met my husband. The moment stays with you for ever – it has that sepia slow-motion "filter" applied. You can rerun it again and again, it's stored in the top shelf of your memory bank.

But love at first sight can happen more than once. The first time I set foot in London I fell hard in love, and I knew that it was for ever. I arrived in late August 2000, knowing no one and nothing, having never been to the UK before. All I had been aware of as I was leaving an international school in Eindhoven, a small town in the Netherlands, was that I was coming to London to study law.

Walking down from my hall of residence in Tavistock Square towards the London School of Economics, tucked away in Aldwych, I fell into a trance – everything moved fast but slow, everything basked in the warm glow of the late-summer sun… It felt as if the sun was shining just to welcome me to this new city, this new beginning. I was attacked by a mad squirrel walking through Russell Square, and nearly got hit by a car, coming at me from the "wrong side", on each of the seven road crossings on my way. What struck me about my new love was its undeniable life force. Each breath of the congested air somehow filled your entire form, each and every cell, with possibility. London was a chrysalis of opportunities, a vast playing field for the curious, brave and reckless.

London set the pace of our love affair – it has been a roller coaster, it has had a million facets and it holds many more in store. It has at times left me exhausted, but never bored. I returned every time I tried to leave; my affairs with Moscow, Amsterdam, Tel Aviv and São Paulo were mere flirtations, serving only to further cement my devotion to London.

London is a juxtaposition – that's why I will never stop loving it. It allows you to be whoever you want to be. For a long time I was a high-flying City lawyer with a penchant for the underground music scene, combining weekend-long squat parties in Plough Yard with Monday meetings on the 30th floor of my firm's offices in Canary Wharf…"transitioning" on the Underground – London's very own "metamorphosis tunnel"; a strange comfort in the knowledge that this is a place where you can always find a creature more bizarre than yourself.

In my 16 years in London I have lived and worked in over 20 locations, ranging from Neasden to Ladbroke Grove to London Fields, which is where I reside now. I haven't even scratched the surface of this city… How apt that my current place of work – a law firm rather than a nightclub – should be in Gough Square, right next to Dr Johnson's house – he of the familiar quote, "Why, Sir, you find no man, at all intellectual, who is willing to leave London. No, Sir, when a man is tired of London, he is tired of life; for there is in London all that life can afford."

Simon Russell Beale

Actor, author and music historian

WATERLOO BRIDGE AND THE THEATRE OF LONDON

I'm writing this in the London Library, which would definitely be one of my favourite places in London. It's still a lending library. There's this tiny little frontage, yet inside there are miles of books across various rooms: it's a little TARDIS. That's good old English amateurism at its best – "yes, do take these wonderful old books out and please bring them back".

The thing I find most special about London, however – clichéd as it might be – is standing on Waterloo Bridge. It's particularly important to me, because I can see the National Theatre from there. I was in New York a few years ago doing a Simon Stephens play called *Bluebird*, about a taxi driver working in London. In the final climactic scene, he talks to his wife about when they were at their happiest, and he mentions going to the theatre, walking across Waterloo Bridge. I remember being in America in the heat of the summer, and I was surrounded by an American cast, to whom it meant nothing. To me, it was home.

Every other year I go back to the National Theatre and do a play: when I'm there, it's my home; my dressing room becomes my office. I worked there for the first time in the mid-1990s, doing a Ben Jonson play with Michael Gambon. It had been on the edge of my consciousness before then, and I had been asked to go, but

I had turned them down, rather grandly. The Jonson play was my first experience of acting there, and I've been performing there ever since. That's more than 20 years now.

If I were to say something about London more generally, it is that it has the best theatre culture in the world. I think it's absolutely extraordinary.

I think, rather dully, that the mixed economy in British theatre – difficult and complex though it is – is a very interesting thing, because you have these great subsidised theatres of different sizes: the Almeida, the National, the RSC, and you've got the West End. So you have *Harry Potter* in the West End competing with a Chekhov play that's on at the National, in the subsidised sector. I think it's the economics of it, oddly enough, that produces the enormous variety. When we had to beg for private money for theatre, we thought it was the end of the world, and it hasn't been. Thankfully people who help subsidise theatre have more sense than to determine what the people inside the industry do.

I went to the Royal Court last night and saw a play – it was an odd, strange, comic, baroque play, and I was surrounded by lots of people in their 20s and 30s, thinking, "This isn't meant for me, but I am loving it." Just extraordinary.

PHIL RYAN

DAYS OUT IN LONDON

What makes London great? Like many Londoners I often wrestle with a love-hate relationship with my London. It is a place of incredible diversity. From people to incomes to cultures. It can be a difficult place to exist. But London somehow accommodates them all. Just. Including me. Many of the favourite projects I have been involved with in my career (so far) have been London based with a London flavour. From helping to set up *The Big Issue* to creating the 12 Bar Club to mounting *The Phil Ryan Show*, London has been the launch pad for such ideas to ripple outwards. However, I think the best way to give you a better handle on my view is by describing a few of my favourite days out. I take many of my friends from abroad along. These are not the typical tourist-destination days out, although any tourist would love them. I think they are my real London. Great London.

You start on the South Bank having a morning crepe and tea, then wandering along the river to Westminster, waving at Big Ben and jumping on a bus up to Trafalgar Square to take in the National Portrait Gallery, turning into Chinatown for a quick noodle lunch, falling into Soho or Covent Garden for some shopping, checking out musical instruments in Denmark Street, then grabbing the tube to Hampstead for a walk on the wild forested heathlands. What other city can offer that palette? Another day starts with breakfast in Borough Market, sampling gastronomic tastes and flavours to make your legs give way. A brisk walk by the river and a bus over Tower Bridge and you're in the 11th-century Tower of London. Then you can try the 21st century by taking a river cruise up to Canary Wharf. Lunch in one of the countless snazzy restaurants around the City and then either whiz across on the cable car to Greenwich or nip onto the Tube and head for Liverpool Street to a gem of a building called Dennis Severs' House, 18 Folgate Street, where you can fall back a few centuries. Then finish off with dinner in Brick Lane, having an amazing curry.

That's only two of my days out. (Sometimes I just take sandwiches!)

London is changing. Many of my favourite places are disappearing. Especially the eccentric and eclectic. Change. Sometimes, not always, for the good, with giant buildings flying up, filling the skylines and cramming more people in. But cities do change. It's in their nature, I guess. I like to think that London has an irrepressible soul, which resides in its people. The folk who make it run and hum and breathe. Its creativity floods across the world. Music, theatre, art, fashion, technology, engineering. You name it, it's made in London. Just like me.

MUSICIAN, WRITER AND ENTREPRENEUR; CO-FOUNDER OF THE BIG ISSUE AND THE 12 BAR CLUB

Jason Sandy

Mudlarker

WHEN THE TIDE RECEDES...

Only in London can you casually stroll along the tidal River Thames and discover truly amazing traces of people who lived here centuries ago.

Several years ago I took my Dad mudlarking along the Thames foreshore while he was visiting London. As we were walking along the river's edge in Central London, we stumbled upon a small face peering out of the black mud. As I carefully lifted the object up, we realised that it was a delicately carved piece of bone. When we showed it to the Museum of London, the historians confirmed that it was a Roman bone hairpin. They dated it to about AD 43–100 based on the ornate female face carved at the top of the long pin.

How exciting to think that the last person to touch this object was a Roman woman living in Londinium almost 2,000 years ago! Judging by the skilfully crafted pin which was found close to the previous site of the Roman governor's palace, I imagine that she was a woman of distinction with elaborately braided hair, held in place with long, elegant pins which displayed her wealth and status. Perhaps a strong gust of wind dislocated the hairpin as the woman was walking along the river's edge.

It is an incredible feeling to discover and hold an artefact knowing that the last person to touch the object lived two millennia ago. What a thrill experiencing hands-on history! Unlike objects kept behind glass in museums, which can only be observed from an impersonal distance, the Thames foreshore allows anyone to touch and feel history for themselves.

Only accessible at low tide for a couple of hours a day, this unique part of London is a tranquil, quiet environment, completely detached from urban life. As the murky waters slowly recede and flow towards the sea at low tide, the exposed foreshore becomes an enchanting and mystical place where time has stopped. The river bed is an eclectic mixture of rocks, oyster shells, broken glass, bricks, terracotta tiles, animal bones, sand, gravel and mud. Hidden within this terrain are historical artefacts deposited or dropped into the river centuries ago, waiting to be discovered and reveal long-lost stories. We are not able to travel back in time, but by finding something like this, untouched since it was lost hundreds or even thousands of years ago, we develop a deep, tangible connection to our past, our city and the personal lives of our forefathers.

As the longest archaeological site in Britain, the Thames foreshore contains an incredible number of historic objects, some of which even predate London's existence. Each one, whether mundane or extraordinary, tells us something unique about London's history.

When the tide is out, you can walk along the foreshore for miles, experiencing London from an unusual and exhilarating viewpoint.

Charles Saumarez Smith

**Cultural historian; Secretary and Chief Executive
of the Royal Academy of Arts**

—

LIMEHOUSE

—

I'm a long-standing resident and lover of East London, that part of the town which lies beyond the old City walls and the Tower of London, and stretches out towards the old docks and now Canary Wharf. I used to explore it in the early 1970s when the two great Hawksmoor churches, St George-in-the-East and St Anne's Limehouse, towered over a landscape of empty docks, social housing, the Regent's Canal and Limehouse Basin.

We moved to Limehouse in the early 1980s, to Newell Street by St Anne's Passage, opposite an old naval training school. There was still a residue of the old Chinese community in the local restaurants – Friends in Salmon Lane, which was in *The Good Food Guide*, and the old Peking restaurant closer to the docks, where one could choose what one wanted to eat out of the fish tanks as one entered.

Changes were beginning. Michael von Clemm, a friend of ours, came looking for storage facilities for La Gavroche, the restaurant he had helped establish with Michel and Albert Roux. He recognised the docks' potential for a new office development modelled on what was happening along the harbour in Boston.

Over the last 30 years, we have seen amazing changes in East London: new roads, new housing, the Docklands Light Railway and the Limehouse Link Tunnel. Canary Wharf now towers over the area like a version of Chicago and there is a cable car over the Thames. But I still get a frisson when I go beyond the Tower and enter a different country, rougher and less built-up, with a history of poverty and shipping, where ships set out for India, Australia and Canton.

Sir Paul Smith

Fashion designer

—

LONDON ABOVE EYE LEVEL

—

I'm blessed with having eyes that look and see: many people have eyes that look but they don't really see. My Dad was an amateur photographer and the founder member of the local photography club in Nottingham. From the age of eleven I was given a camera and every Thursday I used to go to camera-club meetings where people would talk about composition and perspective; I learned a lot about looking through viewfinders and the composition of shots at a very young age. So I suppose my eyes got trained to look at things in an inquisitive way.

I take pictures every day of my life. I'm a very curious person, so I tend to look up as well as at eye level. This morning I took a photograph of a building and posted it on Instagram, saying, "Look up in London; there are so many beautiful things to see. Here's the Grand Trunk Railway building." Someone replied and said, "Just by looking up you can see some of the history of the buildings and the great architecture." I always do this and bump into folks looking down and reading on their phones. There are so many amazing buildings in London that have been created over the years and unfortunately so many people spend their time looking at their smartphones and don't really see what's there.

If you walk down Oxford Street, for instance, most of the shop fronts are dreadful and very of the moment – all advertising hoardings and Perspex. If you do the same journey but look up instead of at eye level, suddenly you see the top of Corinthian columns; you see cherubs,

sculptures… If you go to the top of the offices opposite the Liberty building, you'll see that the tops of the buildings are magnificent. Unfortunately, nowadays, property developers are building as deep as they can, as high as they can, for as low cost as they can. Previously people could build to impress and create a symbol for their company. Just look at the BBC building in Portland Place, or the amazing Nash terrace that runs up and into Regent's Park (and that once began in Regent Street).

Looking above eye level is like discovering a secret world, and that's one of the aspects I love most about London: its secrets. There are so many secrets that people don't know about. There's the pet cemetery on the edge of Hyde Park, where the park meets Bayswater Road; there's a Victorian tunnel under the Thames; the whispering gallery at St Paul's… Near where the Photographers' Gallery used to be, between Charing Cross Road and St Martin's Lane, there is a little theatre – on the wall there's a hook where policemen who were doing traffic control used to hang their cloaks. It's still there, to this day. And one of the things that are easy to forget – though it's not really a secret – is how many parks there are in London. When people from my Japanese office come over they can't believe how many parks there are, like Holland Park, with its rabbits, peacocks and squirrels – it's like being in the countryside.

It's all there if you just look for it. So go on, do it: start looking up!

Cassandra Stavrou

Founder of Propercorn

—

THE WELCOMING AND FOSTERING OF ENTREPRENEURIALISM

—

My family moved to London from Cyprus 60 years ago. Inspirited by the pace and dynamism of this incredible city, they started their own businesses. They soon joined a diverse community of entrepreneurs and businesspeople, all spurred on by London's unwavering ability to inspire and nurture new ideas.

From local corner shops offering goods from around the globe, to Old Street roundabout's onslaught of tech start-ups, London cultivates enterprise. If you have an idea that may change your community, or even change the world, it is in London that it can take flight.

When I decided to start my own business, I knew that its story had to begin in my hometown. As a Londoner, the soul of this city is woven into me; I have come to meet the brilliant and inspiring young people who call our capital home, and who I knew would be vital in helping build my own business.

That business was making popcorn! For most people that seems a simple enterprise. But doing it well is a huge challenge. Luckily, and with a lot of hard work, our popcorn has found its way into the offices and homes of not only Londoners, but consumers across Europe. On reflection it was London that played an integral part in our company's journey. Our brand is a representation of the trends, colours, flavours and dynamism that make up the greatest city in the world.

You never stop discovering London. Most recently it is the Regent's Canal that has offered me a new adventure. The walk eastwards along this historic waterway from King's Cross to Broadway Market is a window into a city that embraces its past but always will excite, challenge and progress. In those few miles you can buy freshly shucked oysters from a hole in the wall, eat in cafés built into once abandoned warehouses, buy a novel from a floating bookshop on a converted barge, and peer into artists' studios.

That very canal is now home to our first proper HQ! It seemed fitting that, as the company needed a new home, we would move here – a perfect place for the creativity of our staff and the culture of our company to start its next chapter.

John Updike wrote that cities "aren't like people, they live on and on". In a way we are all temporary custodians of the places where we choose to live and work. I feel immensely fortunate that my story, and that of my company, is being shaped in this of all cities.

VINEGAR STROKES

The Whoopi Goldberg of Drag

—

BUS STOPS AND TUBE STATIONS

—

I've always said, "It's impossible to get lost in London. You will always lose yourself to a bus stop or Tube station to get you where you need to go."

And how true that is – well, it is for me, anyway.

But that applied to me so much more than being physically lost. I now see it as a metaphor for a time when I was lost in my life. I felt like I had just been scattered around the capital and I was now trying to find all the pieces to put them back together.

My Confidence was knocked into a wall in the streets of East London.

My Drive was drinking in a dark bar in South London.

My Relationships were lying in pieces in West London.

My Creativity was six feet under somewhere in North London.

And there I was in the centre of it all, completely *lost*!

So, I began looking for bus stops and Tube stations.

After accepting that my creativity might need some reinvention and that I needed to tap into what really made me tick, my bus stops and Tube stations led me to the unexpected world of cabaret, stand-up comedy and drag.

My second ever time performing in drag took me to the Royal Vauxhall Tavern, one of the most iconic LGBT venues in London. So many great names have passed through the doors and performed on the RVT stage – Lily Savage, Dame Edna, even Princess Diana and Freddie Mercury went in for a drink and a dance.

The first time I stepped up on the RVT stage I finally felt like I was in a familiar place. I performed ten minutes of songs and stand-up comedy and behind the blinding glow of the spotlight the audience clapped, cheered and laughed. Since then I haven't looked back. Slowly but surely I found my Confidence, rediscovered my Drive, built new Relationships as well as mending old ones and revived my Creativity – and this is all thanks to a little pub with a stage, some lights and a microphone.

The Royal Vauxhall Tavern represents so much of the ideals of what London is to me. It's a place that breathes Creativity, Art, Acceptance, Opportunity, Entertainment, Inspiration, Culture, Passion, Community, Support, Encouragement.

London for me is a place of opportunity and new beginnings at any time when I feel a little lost.

Just look for those bus stops or Tube stations and you're bound to lose yourself to a new and exciting place in life that you were not expecting.

Deyan Sudjic

Writer and broadcaster; Director of the Design Museum

A MORNING WALK THROUGH REGENT'S PARK

I live in a house in Camden caught between two very different incarnations of London. Five minutes to the east are the tattoo parlours of Camden Market, which offer to pierce every conceivable part of the body. During the day, the streets are crammed with an endless flow of visitors. On Saturday nights there is broken glass and vomit on the pavement. The hostel that George Orwell described in *Down and Out in Paris and London* is not far away. This is the London that Dickens depicted in *Dombey and Son*, cut in two by the coming of the railways, leaving fractured streets perched on the edge of embankments.

On the other side of the street, John Nash's sublime Regent's Park is just a few steps away.

We have convinced ourselves that London, set beside Paris or Berlin, doesn't go in for grand plans, that it is the product of a series of overgrown villages organically growing together.

To judge by the astonishing agglomeration of cranes that are lining both sides of the Thames from Stratford in the east to Battersea in the west, London is certainly much more ruthless about its future than that comfortable myth would suggest.

And it was John Nash's campaign at the start of the 19th century to transform Central London for his patron, the Prince Regent, that inspired Napoleon III, in exile in Britain, to rebuild Paris when he eventually got home.

Nash created Regent's Park, and worked on the road layouts that stretched all the way south to Buckingham Palace, by way of Portland Place, Regent Street, the Haymarket, Trafalgar Square and the Mall.

The park is a defining piece of picturesque city planning. It was originally planned to have a scattering of villas in the green lawns at its centre, and was edged by a series of grand stucco-faced terraces that gave individual houses the aspect of palaces.

Nash designed a number of the terraces himself, deploying giant classical orders, pediments and rooftop sculpture, but much of the housing was developed by builders buying plots of land. Some of these deliberately flouted Nash's stylistic guidelines, which accounts for the sudden shift from sandstone French Empire style to white stucco classicism to grey brick gothic along the eastern edge.

On summer mornings crossing Regent's Park is the perfect way to start a day at work, a 15-minute walk across rolling grass meadows, past heroically scaled terraces, past the house in which Nash himself lived and Denys Lasdun's Royal College of Physicians, one of the best of the landmarks of the 1960s.

It's a model of all that a city can be, offering a contemplative moment in the midst of grandeur.

Pips Taylor

TV presenter

LEAKE STREET

For me, one of the best parts of London is hidden just out of sight. If you pop down a little side street near the arches, it will take you under the train tracks of Waterloo Station. There you will find Leake Street. Informally known as the Banksy Tunnel, it is a safe haven for graffiti artists honing their skills.

As you enter, you can hear the shaking cans…that sharp clap of a sound as the metal ball gets thrown around the inside of the canister – it's almost calming. Artists at work. For me this is a haven of creativity, layers upon layers of art, each day reworked, re-covered and refashioned.

I first came across this place a few years back. Armed with a camera, I chatted to the street artists. For the most part they don't want to be found and documented, they want to be left in their creative zone, oblivious to the sharp tang from the paint that almost chokes you as you enter the tunnel. There's something quite exciting about leaving your mark down here… so I set to work on tagging my name… I felt excitement, like I was doing something naughty – but I wasn't! Within minutes my tag was on the tunnel wall. I wandered off, excited to have left my mark, but even more at the idea of how fleeting the experience was.

A tag takes a short amount of time, but often artists work on more complex pieces for over 12 hours. Irrespective of the time taken, the wall will be repainted in a day or two as another artistic creature pops down, sets up for the day and gets to work. Leake Street draws me back again and again to think about how I left my mark on London, a mark that was probably gone by the next morning. For me, that's rather magical. It reminds me not to take city life too seriously. Sure, we all want to make our mark, but in a city of close to 9 million it's good to remember how fleeting that mark might be.

MARIA THOMAS

LONDON IS A JOURNEY

London is a journey; a rocky road; you tweet, you text, you write a status. You stay in that shiny bubble and it doesn't matter what religion/race/sexuality or gender you are. The unwritten rule is to stick to your own. My name is Eeman and this is my journey through London, through Islam, through the great in Great Britain.

I like to talk so I never shut up: I like to write – it's a release; I like to touch things which meet my sensory needs. Don't get me wrong – I like to fight! But I'll only ever fight for my rights, for the rights of others. When relationships break down, it hurts. You become homeless and you fall into Central London; Centrepoint holds you long enough to get you on your feet. You meet the love of your life and you settle down. Then you do the one thing every girl wants: you discover the world of Islam and you marry. You're still damaged, but all you see is culture and beauty. The Islamic way is beautiful, but the culture can be oppressive. The British way is to have fun and down your wine, but when it's every single weekend, you're labelled.

The London way is to IGNORE; don't look, don't stare and definitely don't touch! But that's just how we like it, right?

I live in what you'd call temporary accommodation, but I love people enough not to leave. I want to stay, but I'm stuck. You look around you and you educate yourself; go to school, go to university, just live! Then you become confused, scared, paranoid and angry. You lash out and you get locked up; the police take you, but not to jail, of course – to hospital.

You switch your label: no longer homeless. Woo hooooo! Just mentally ill. They call it polymorphic psychotic disorder. I call it being a Mum to Hope.

YOUNG LONDONER HELPED BY HOMELESSNESS CHARITY **CENTREPOINT**

Charlotte Tilbury

Make-up artist

PORTOBELLO ROAD

The area I love most in London is Notting Hill. Portobello Road. It's home.

I've lived here for 25 years. It's part of the tapestry of my life – I have so many friends, experiences and magical moments from Portobello Road. It's a constantly evolving, energetic and beautiful place where amazing artists and eccentric characters converge.

I love exploring its treasure troves of trinkets in the vintage stores, the buzz of the market, summer sun-kissed drinks in the evening light at sunset, playing with my boys in the park across the road from me… the list is endless.

There's something timeless and magical about the area – it's full of style, fun, and beauty!

It also holds so many memories for me – that's the incredible thing. Monumental memories: from buying myself my first house to bringing my babies back from the hospital to having infamous parties in my kitchen; even conceptualizing the bones of my brand before I even had a product to my name…. There are too many to say!

Portobello Road makes me feel inspired. It is iconic, a theatre of characters and performers – a place where no one is inhibited. There is such a bubbling mix of everyone and everything – it never gets boring. It serves as daily inspiration for everything.

I would recommend anyone to go and immerse themselves there! Potter down Portobello on a Friday or a Saturday morning, because you will be the first to get the best bargains and buys of the market. Eat delicious truffle pasta in Essenza for lunch, bury yourself in vintage Ossie Clarke in One of a Kind, Found and Vision and Rellik – it's the best vintage shopping ever! You can even have Mairead Lewin come and style you with her incredible vintage finds, as she does for so many celebrities. Meander down Golborne Road, and take in Ernö Goldfinger's Trellick Tower…. There is so much to do and see….

For me, the DNA of Portobello is representative of London at its best. It is an eclectic melting pot of characters from different walks of life and cultures. It's a celebration of creativity, diversity, freedom of expression, and joy. It has an edge, which is what makes life exciting. It is immersive, surreal and beautiful….

SETH TROXLER

MULTICULTURAL LONDON

I travel the world for a living, being a DJ, and there are so few places that have the levels of acceptance and tolerance that London has. This city attracts so many people – a lot of people from other cultures came here back in colonial times and started trading.

I'm not a historian, so I don't know about the story of immigration and I'm no expert, but from a visual point of view, East London in particular is the most integrated area that I've experienced in London. It's also where I've always based myself when I'm in town, around the Barbican area, Farringdon – that's where I spend most of my time in London. One of my favourite current spots is Dalston: it is such a cross-section of society, I find it really inspiring seeing all kinds of people living together and accepting each other.

I think it is that which makes London so remarkable: its multiculturalism, and out of every other place in the world with mixed culture, it works. That's the thing I find the most fascinating about here, and what I love about the city so much.

I've been spending a lot more time in and around London for the last few years, but I'd been coming here for years before that. I originally came here for a girl; she broke up with me, but I kept coming back. It's the most diverse society. Whether it's people of different colour or whatever sexual orientation, you get to see every type of person, and everyone congregates, no matter what class, in this one place. You celebrate life together.

I'm American and there is more racial tension over there, but here everything just gels. It's a beautiful unification. It's the greatest city.

DJ AND **MUSIC PRODUCER**; JOINT-OWNER OF **SMOKEY TAILS RESTAURANT** IN SHOREDITCH

Sophie Walker

Journalist, author, campaigner for diversity and disability awareness and leader of the Women's Equality Party

—

LONDON AS LAYERS OF LIFE

—

London is all the layers of my life.

As I move about the city they press around me.

Sometimes, the Tube doors will peel back and remind me of a place I was ten years ago. Other days, a glance down from the bus window picks out a forgotten spot. There are evenings when the end of a street, glimpsed from the back of a passing cab, lights a memory.

These are some of the layers.

There is a layer that is Camden Market, where I bought printed T-shirts and thought I was the coolest teenager of the thousands there, inhaling patchouli and spices on a bleary Sunday morning.

There is a layer that is Wong Kei's restaurant in Chinatown, where the staff was legendarily rude and my friends and I would giggle on Saturday nights as we were snapped at over pork dumplings.

There is a paper-thin layer – a tattered thing – that is the door that used to lead down to the Dive Bar, with its dark corners and sticky table tops and murmured conversations lasting long into late nights.

There's a layer that is Cable Street, now seen mainly from a rattling train that winds around and past the tower block where I used to live. If I peer up I can see the ex-council flat on the 22nd floor with the balcony from which I looked out over the city in May 1997, and watched fireworks go off with every Labour constituency win.

There are several layers in Hackney: from the hospital in Homerton where I watched the dark sky turn pink until it was time to meet my upside-down, awkward first-born; to the park in Stoke Newington that I circled grimly for hours as she yelled at me from a blue pram.

There are layers more – in Westminster and Canary Wharf (these ones are brittle, set by long hours of office work and ambition); on the Strand (these are rosy-tinted, from the night I met my husband, and a waiter in Simpson's stirred love into our vodka martinis); in the temporary unit of an autism diagnosis clinic in Edgware (these ones are close to the surface and a bit damp with tears; they are the ones that have formed me most recently).

I am setting down new layers right now – in a dingy office that has a hole in the roof and windows that rattle when the trains pass – while I work on a huge and simple idea about a political party for equality.

I love London because every day it shows me how far I have come, and thus how far I can go.

ALICE WILLIAMS

Founder of the Luminary Bakery, which provides training for vulnerable women

—

ROAD SWEEPERS

—

A police officer once told me, "If you want to know what happened, ask a road sweeper, because they see everything." Those hard workers graft away on London's streets generally unappreciated and unnoticed, and can observe the goings-on utterly undetected.

I open up a café on Brick Lane at the crack of dawn, and it's usually just me and the road sweepers awake. They are busy cleaning up the carnage of the night before – beer bottles, laughing-gas canisters, salt-beef droppings and all manner of unidentified liquids – getting the streets ready for whatever activities today will behold.

That is what I love about London – you've just got no idea what spectacles await you.

Daily I am surprised by interesting characters, celebrity sightings, bizarre vehicles, unexpected protests, innovative hustling techniques, replacement buses and random pop-ups. People

of all world views, languages, ethnicities and religions cross paths here and they each bring something interesting.

London's rich history and contradictory economic potential bring tourists and settlers from all over the world, which has led to the beautiful fusion of cultures and cuisines we can now enjoy in easy proximity.

Serving customers in such an eclectic area, I get to meet people from all walks of life; their stories are fascinating. We can learn so much from the old East Ender, the Bangladeshi shop owner, the French art student and especially the road sweeper.

London is uniquely positioned for all of these people to live in harmony. My favourite thing above all? When instead of ignorance and hatred, I see this breeding love, respect and understanding.

Martine Wright

7/7 victim; GB representative at the London 2012 Olympic Games
—

LONDON – MADE BY PEOPLE AND PASSION
—

It is interesting to try to define what makes a city great, and what makes it stand out from others. Is it how it contributes to moments in world history or maybe its famous landmarks? Different people will see it in a different way; for me it has always been about the people and a place I will always call home.

I am proud to say that I am a genuine cockney, born within the sound of Bow Bells at St Bartholomew's Hospital in the City, as are all my family who grew up in the heart of London, with my Mum and Dad experiencing London at war at a very young age. There are not many people that you know who can still remember the sound of the sirens and being taken down into the Tube station shelter to be protected from the bombs of the Blitz (apart from the one that fell through the roof onto my Nan's sofa – unexploded, thankfully!). Nor are there many who can tell you, like my Dad did, how he used to tie barrage balloons to his bike and see how far he could drag these across the squares of London.

I've always loved to people-watch, so when I was commuting into my office on 6 July 2005 I felt a sense of anticipation, even nervousness in the air: this was the day it would be announced whether or not London had won the Olympic and Paralympic bid. As if by magic, a few hours later we were all celebrating a famous victory in London boozers with so many other Londoners. We had won: the Olympics and Paralympics were actually coming to London, when Paris had been tipped to win. All I kept thinking was, "I need to get tickets to this as I am a Londoner and born just a few miles away from the stadium and sports park that will be built."

This award in itself was recognition of what a great city London is and showed what we could offer, in terms of organisation, hospitality and reliability, among other qualities. We were rightly proud.

The next morning, 7 July, changed everything for London, and for myself and the people who live here. I was sat just over a metre away from a suicide bomber on the Aldgate Tube train, and the impact of the bomber's blast was a turning point in my life. Having narrowly survived, I witnessed then the spirit of people, the spirit of London, and what I believe personifies our city. From those who risked their lives in saving others, to those who held hands and comforted victims and families that had lost loved ones, and those who came in off the streets to offer up blood in emergency centres, London came together that day. The resilience shown by its people from all walks of life and from all communities made a statement that we would not be deterred or beaten.

Roll on seven years, and after an extended period of rehabilitation, learning to walk again and resetting my life goals, I came to be one of the thousands of athletes who took part in the London 2012 Games. It was not just my injuries and physical changes that saw me in a position to be lining up with team-mates to enter the stadium for the Paralympic Games opening ceremony, but the dedication, belief and support of my fellow Londoners that allowed me to refocus and retrain to become an elite athlete.

For me this was a journey I think I was always meant to make, just like my journey into the world as a Bow Bells cockney, just like the journeys I used

to make in my Dad's black taxi and the journey I was making that fateful morning. I believe the whole reason why I was involved in the atrocities of 7/7 was ultimately to make the positive journey back to London, my hometown, to take place in the biggest sporting show on earth.

And what was London 2012 remembered for? What would the lasting image be? An Olympic Stadium or city, a bagful of medals? No, something more, much more. The people and their passion for London. Our Games Makers were an army of volunteers from all over London and beyond, bringing together a dizzy cocktail of skills, enthusiasm, energy. The support we received from the nation and the millions of people lining the streets to wave banners and congratulate us in our victory parade placed the Paralympics firmly as an event of ability and excellence on the world map.

Our city changed for a month. We talked to each other on the Tube, we found time to get to know each other and we shared the common bond that was not just sport, but a new-found friendship based on respect and trust.

It was the people of London who helped to put the events of 7/7 behind us and allowed us as a large, diverse, yet cohesive community to move on. For me it represented a real paradox. From being in the wrong place at the wrong time in 2005, I ended up being in the right place at the right time at the Paralympic Games in my hometown of London in 2012.

My best memory from that time? It was the people and their passion, from my family and friends to my team-mates and all the Games Makers and volunteers who made it happen. The amazing support we received from the whole nation and from my fellow Londoners showed that it takes people and their passion to make a city.

My London. Your London. Our London.

Peter York

**Cultural commentator and co-author
of *The Official Sloane Ranger Handbook***

THE PICCADILLY LINE

When I was given the Piccadilly Line to write a book about – as part of Penguin's series celebrating 150 years of the London Underground in 2013 – I found I'd forgotten almost everything I'd ever known about the Tube. I hadn't been on it for about 25 years. I might very well have said I liked the Piccadilly Line because its livery, that darkish, slightly purply blue, the blue of rosettes and fancy ribbons, was the nicest colour on Harry Beck's famous Tube map of 1933. Or I could have said that it had the nicest, most evocative name. Of the four Tube lines whose names actually celebrate London places, the Piccadilly is the grandest and the most specific. Piccadilly is a real street right at the centre, with two marvellous places – Mayfair and St James's – to either side.

When Helen Conford, Penguin's editor of the Tube series, allocated me my subject, she said she'd kept the nicest line for me. I thought, "I bet she says that to all the boys."

Eight months of over-researching later – including, obviously, a lot of Tube-riding – I knew she'd been right. I'd come to the conclusion that the Tube as a whole and its history were completely wonderful. But also that the Piccadilly Line was the best bit.

The Piccadilly Line at its core – the short stretch from South Kensington to Piccadilly Circus planned by its original sponsors in 1901 – traversed the shortest, sweetest, smartest, most central bit of London imaginable. It delivered extreme urban magic through its locations (by the time it actually opened, in 1906, it had been extended from Hammersmith to the west to Finsbury Park in the north). But in its later, suburban extensions in the early 1930s the Piccadilly Line, reaching out to some pretty unglamorous locations (Hounslow, Bounds Green!), took with it the extraordinary bounty of Charles Holden's station architecture.

Charles Holden's "British modernist" style was at the core of the London Underground's deserved reputation as Britain's greatest public-art patron of the 20th century. Frank Pick, the CEO of the Underground both as a commercial company and later as a publicly owned one from 1933 until he died in 1941, became an increasingly convinced proselytiser and patron for British modern art and architecture. In 1930 he and Holden had made a pilgrimage to Northern Europe – Germany and Scandinavia – to see the reality of the "built Bauhaus" and other European avant-gardery. Out of that came the 48 modernist stations that Holden built for the London Underground as a whole. The largest single group of these and – in 1930s terms – some of the most spectacular were the 24 he designed for the Piccadilly Line. Arnos Grove, say, or Southgate must have looked like spaceships – they both have circular plans – dropped in the centre of rows of developer housing, semis that were still being built practically to Edwardian styles. These new

stations were embassies of modernity, with the amazing promise that they could reliably deliver commuters from the suburbs to "town" in half an hour or less. To cinemas, theatres, department stores and restaurants – the magic world of the modern city centre. And at the very centre of

the line is an Art Deco marvel, one that warrants a fancy restoration: Piccadilly Circus Station. With its circular design echoing that of Piccadilly Circus above it, it is the Underground counterpart to Arnos Grove or Southgate. You haven't done London if you haven't done the Piccadilly Line.

About the author

Conrad Gamble is a writer and performance poet. He, unsurprisingly, lives in London.

A thank you

From the moment my mind grabbed hold of this idea I never doubted that it would happen. There are many to thank for helping it be realised. My publisher Octopus, the lovely Hannah Knowles, who has been great throughout, and latterly Leanne Bryan. My fantastic agent Janelle Andrew. My two main photographers, Tony Briggs and Andy Donohoe. Their positive spirit has wonderfully reflected the ethos of this idea, they have been fantastic company and produced sparkling results. A big thank you to Rowly Bourne, who was very helpful at the genesis of the project. To my brother, whom I love dearly and who has helped me through some extremely tough times, and to my mother who is never less than amazing and to whom I owe so much. I love you.

Picture credits

7, 9, 11, 13, 15, 16, 18–19 Andy Donohoe; 21, 22 Tony Briggs; 25, 27, 29 Andy Donohoe; 31 Tony Briggs; 33 Ben Ottewell, reproduced courtesy of Sam Bompass; 36 Tony Briggs; 39 Andy Donohoe; 41 Sin Bozkurt, reproduced courtesy of Vicky Butterfly; 43, 45 Andy Donohoe; 47 Jack Andrew Davison, reproduced courtesy of Sadie Coles; 49 Tony Briggs; 51, 53, 55 Andy Donohoe; 57a, 57b Tony Briggs; 58 Stephanie Dennington; 61 Andy Donohoe; 63 Tony Briggs; 65 Robbie Lawrence, reproduced courtesy of Alex Eagle; 66 David X Green; 69 Hal Shinnie, reproduced courtesy of Ben Eliot; 71, 73, 75 Tony Briggs; 77 Andy Donohoe; 79 Tony Briggs; 81 Andy Donohoe; 83 Hannah Hillier, reproduced courtesy of Olivia Grant; 85 Andy Donohoe; 89, 90 Tony Briggs; 93 Steve Double, reproduced courtesy of Dame Zaha Hadid; 95, 97al, 97ar, 97bl, 97br Tony Briggs; 99 Andy Donohoe; 101 Andrew Woffinden, reproduced courtesy of Anya Hindmarch; 102 Andy Donohoe; 105 Mariano Vivanco, reproduced courtesy of Henry Holland; 107, 109, 111 Andy Donohoe; 113, 114 Dean Chalkely, reproduced courtesy of Norman Jay; 117 Tony Briggs; 119 Sudhir Pithy; 121 Andy Donohoe; 123 Tony Briggs; 125 main Edu Torres; 125b Tony Briggs; 127 Andy Donohoe; 129a, 129b Joe Garcia, reproduced courtesy of Charles Landry; 131, 133 Andy Donohoe; 135 Eddie Otchere, reproduced courtesy of Don Letts; 137 Phil Sharpe, reproduced courtesy of Ben Lambert and Natasha Coleman; 139, 140 Andy Donohoe; 143 Tony Briggs; 145 Andy Donohoe; 147, 149 Tony Briggs; 151 Rory Lindsay, reproduced courtesy of Tatiana Mercer; 153 Dai Williams; 155, 157 Andy Donohoe; 159 Charlie Wheeler; 161 Ammar Darwish, reproduced courtesy of David Nott; 163, 165 Tony Briggs; 167 Nicholas Ashley, reproduced courtesy of Grace Pilkington; 168, 171 Andy Donohoe; 173 Tony Briggs; 175 Derek Dsouza; 177 Andy Donohoe; 179 Tony Briggs; 181 Sarah Lee; 183 Andy Donohoe; 185 Tony Briggs; 187 David Loftus, reproduced courtesy of Ruth Rodgers; 189 Andy Donohoe; 191 Charlie Carter; 193 Tony Briggs; 195 Andy Donohoe; 197 Tony Briggs; 199 James Mooney, reproduced courtesy of Paul Smith; 201 Cassandra Stavrou; 203, 205 Andy Donohoe; 207 Stephanie Peers, reproduced courtesy of Pips Taylor; 209 Maria Thomas; 213 Axel Pics Photography, reproduced courtesy of Seth Troxler; 214 Tony Briggs; 217, 219 Andy Donohoe; 221 Tony Briggs; 222 Michele Beint.

An Hachette UK Company
www.hachette.co.uk

First published in Great Britain in 2017 by Cassell,
a division of Octopus Publishing Group Ltd
Carmelite House
50 Victoria Embankment
London EC4Y 0DZ
www.octopusbooks.co.uk

Distributed in the US by
Hachette Book Group
1290 Avenue of the Americas
4th and 5th Floors
New York, NY 10020

Distributed in Canada by
Canadian Manda Group
664 Annette St.
Toronto, Ontario, Canada M6S 2C8

ISBN 978-1-84403-921-0

A CIP catalogue record for this book is available from
the British Library.

Printed and bound in Italy.

1 3 5 7 9 10 8 6 4 2

The team (and what *they* love about London)
Commissioning Editor Hannah Knowles (The Wellcome Collection)
Art Director Yasia Williams-Leedham (Greenwich Park)
Senior Editor Leanne Bryan (Exploring the city by bike)
Copy Editor Caroline Taggart (Dean's Yard, Westminster)
Designer Steve Leard (Strand-on-the-Green)
Picture Research Manager Giulia Hetherington
(The vibrant music scene)
Assistant Production Manager Lucy Carter
(The culture, and the variety of cuisines and shops)